The Foundation for Exploration

Sean Goonan

The Foundation Press
www.thefoundationpress.com
thefoundationpress@zoho.com

Contents

Preface

In order to understand what I call "the duality of human nature" you must understand the difference between the words Truth and truth, Wrong and wrong, and Right and right. Truth, Wrong, and Right are objective understandings of existence, an impossibility given our current reality. The words truth, wrong, and right are subjective understandings of existence, and they are what we must work off of. All words capitalized in this essay when they should not be reflect their objectivity or more closeness to objectivity compared to their lowercase counterparts. Objectivity may be the goal, but it is not the key to achieving that goal; subjectivity is the key. A foundational philosophy based in subjectivity is the key to action. It is how you build and it is how you prevent things from decaying.

Introduction

In order for humanity to thrive with people living in true happiness, or for humanity to continue at all, a foundation, or mental and societal structure is necessary. The foundation I have discovered or created is a temporary structure based on the current path and understanding of humanity. It is based off of a single primary question in which everything else is derived off of:

Should I continue to exist?

In which there is no right or wrong answer.

I will argue in this essay that if you want to obtain true happiness and have humanity continue to exist:

A. You must accept that your life is meaningless.
B. You must then create a subjective foundational mental structure to build an enjoyable life and to protect yourself from meaninglessness.
C. You must create a strong foundational societal structure to support individuals.
D. You must understand that some things destroy humanity and other things strengthen humanity.
E. What is "right" or "wrong" depends on the strengthening or destructive qualities of the action or thought.
F. You must accept and work with things that are not absolute truths in order to accomplish B, C, D, and E.
G. You must accept things that cannot be changed but not succumb to their negative consequences.
H. You must build upon things that can be changed in order to create a stronger mental and societal structure and create a better life.

This essay will be focused on realizing the many ways people consciously and unconsciously destroy the quality of their life and the possibility for their existence and how it is necessary to reduce destructive tendencies and encourage other behavior in order to keep existing and thrive.

In order to survive, function, enjoy and self-actualize you must understand your existence and you must create your existence. In order to understand and to build we must explore.

This is the foundation for exploration.

Section 1: Welcome to Not Nothing

Life is meaningless and absurd. We have free will, we are not all powerful, we are not all knowing, and we experience the universe with a biological framework and consciousness. I have discovered that due to this inherent structure of our perceived existence, we follow two distinct paths. The duality of human nature is this:

> Every single human feeling, thought, or action at any level of experience or awareness can be categorized under two equally valid but opposite reactions to the absurdity of the universe. Rejection and destruction or acceptance and building.

Simplistic approximations of the duality are:
The path of destruction is hopelessness and the path of building is hope.
The path of destruction is unrestricted individual freedom and the path of building is discipline.
The path of destruction is ignorance and the path of building seeks to understand life.
The path of destruction leads to extinction and the path of building leads to survival.

Neither reaction to our perceived existence is "better" than the other. It is vital to understand that these reactions are philosophically equal and justified avenues of experience and that these reactions permeate through every moment of our existence. The reactions can have different magnitudes or effects on our lives and the lives of others, but at their core is the same duality, unchanging no matter how miniscule or consequential the instance.

These infinitesimal reactions can be viewed on a polar spectrum with complete destruction or building at either end and everything at a certain level of one or the other between, but they can also be viewed as two distinct paths when viewed over a longer period of time. Changing paths from building to destruction can be done in an instant with a powerful thought or action, but leaving the path of destruction for the path of building takes much longer, requires tremendous effort, and the path of building must always be upheld and maintained. The path of destruction can simply end in you killing yourself, while the path of building means living a deep life of creation, searching and experiencing what life has to offer. Remember that even if you are on the path of destruction, it is always possible to fight out of it and get on the path of building, although the deeper you are in destruction, the harder it is to get out of.

You can accept the meaninglessness of life and go down either path. You can be at the highest philosophical understanding of the universe and go down either path. It is impossible to articulate perfectly why someone should choose to accept life rather than reject it, but I will explain my personal decision. Always remember that the power of choice always rests on you. In order to determine if you want to go on the path of destruction or building, you have to first ask yourself if life is worth living. Destructive thinking, which is not the only option, may cloud one's judgment on the worth of life. I will explain what going down each path entails, and if you choose life, I will explain how you can prosper.

Section 2: Destruction and Building

Life is completely meaningless and free will allows for people to act on the meaninglessness in different ways, all funneling categorically into the duality: Destruction or Building. The path of building builds the collective conscious and everything necessary to support it to enjoy life and discover Truth, while the path of destruction tears everything down. It is not Wrong for people to decide consciously or unconsciously to ruin what others have built because at the core of why people build, there is no absolute Reason to build in the first place. An absence of absolute Reason does not make destruction automatically Right or building automatically futile.

In the duality something that is wrong is actually something that is destructive. Something that is right is something that builds on top of our meaningless existence for a life worth living and strengthens people against destructiveness.

Fundamental individual destructive tendencies given our free will in a meaningless existence are a lack of self-control, cowardice, a lack of wonder, and a lack of sense of humor. Without courage, self-control, wonder and/or humor the individual and society disintegrates. A lack of those four things leads people to wrath, depression, madness, hedonism, and ignorance. These five major ways that destructiveness occurs greatly diminish the quality of someone's life and eventually lead to the cessation of life for the individual and humanity.

All of these reactions influence the collective conscious, which shapes the existence of the individual and humanity.

Individuals create the collective conscious and are created by the collective conscious.
Individuals influence the collective conscious and are influenced by the collective conscious.

Society is an entity that binds and directs individuals according to the perceived collective conscious. It is intertwined with the individual and can create destructiveness in the individual. A collective effort is needed in order for humanity to self-actualize and be on the path of building. Society is the vehicle for building.

Individuals create society and are created by society. Individuals influence society and are influenced by society.

A fundamental way society creates destructiveness in the individual is the creation of powerlessness along with, or due to encouraging the destructive behavior above. Society can destroy individuals by pushing wrath, depression, hedonism, madness, and ignorance onto them, and in turn the collective society is destroyed itself. Everything is connected. An individual may have been courageous and in control and possess humor and wonder if not for the outside force of society pushing the person to be destructive. But remember, an individual may and should always strive to be on the path of building despite all of the wrongness surrounding oneself if the individual chooses life.

Ways of Self and Societal Destruction:

1. Lack of Self-control
2. Lack of Courage
3. Lack of Wonder
4. Lack of Humor

These four things lead the individual to five destructive tendencies:

The Five Destructors

Wrath

Our inherent meaningless existence produces mental and physical anguish. Other people or society as a whole can exacerbate anguish produced by existing. The source of this mental and physical anguish is powerlessness. An individual that feels powerless may reject the conditions that produce the powerlessness and retaliate through wrath as an attempt to gain power. The attempt to gain power through wrath is either the attempt to supersede the powerlessness by trying to obtain all the power one can get (which indirectly creates destructiveness in the individual and society), or the direct destruction of anything that creates powerlessness.

Wrath is destruction and destruction is power.
Wrath is extreme power and extreme power is destruction.

A loss of self-control is the primary reason for acting in wrath, but deficiencies in courage, wonder, and humor play major roles as well. People may consciously or unconsciously be wrathful.

Wrath is not anger. Anger is a powerful tool and emotion that should be used in the path of building. Anger becomes wrath and becomes destructive when one loses control, loses focus, and steps outside of what is productive and necessary for the preservation of society and life.

If wrath occurs naturally in someone when exploring the true nature of their existence, or if it occurs naturally in someone due to outside influences from society and other people, why not be wrathful? One must resist being wrathful because being wrathful is being destructive towards life. Wrath is destructive because it deteriorates the mind, destroys bonds between people, destroys the bond between the individual and the universe that makes life worth living, destroys ideas that preserve and provide a foundation for an enjoyable life, and it directly inflicts unnecessary damage on other people and society. There are consequences for all thoughts, all states of being, and all actions. These internalities and externalitites, or things that occur, influence the collective and subjective planes of existence, which are in constant change. Wrath produces negative consequences for the planes of existence.

When feeling powerless, the choice can be made to relinquish all self-control and act in wrath. This path is chosen to alleviate the suffering because the individual feels backed into a corner with no other options. Any attempt to bargain with others or oneself about the situation is seen as digging oneself further into weakness and despair. Wrath is seen as necessary, Right, effective, and a cathartic release of built up pressure and rage. The danger and destructiveness of wrath is its absoluteness, insatiability, and extremeness.

People are naturally averse to powerlessness. The form of this aversion determines if the individual is in a state of building or destruction. Building is remaining in control of the anger, determining its source, and taking controlled action in deconstructing the source of powerlessness if necessary. The wrathful person loses control over the anger and unleashes destruction. The wrathful individual begins to develop a sense of absoluteness and insatiability in eradicating the powerlessness. The individual may be completely justified in feeling angry and may be justified in venturing a little into a wrathful state, but if that person allows that wrath to take hold then they are down the path of destruction. A person must manage their anger in the initial short term and take short and long term steps in alleviating their suffering. There is no future in wrath.

An individual will naturally feel angry towards feelings of powerlessness, but it is how the individual then deals with the scenario after the feeling of anger that determines if they are destructive or building.

Some forms of powerlessness are natural and unchanging.
The individual must recognize and understand the nature of this powerlessness.
Attempts to eradicate this form of powerlessness are

completely useless and instead it must be worked with.

Some forms of powerlessness are non-existent or blown out of proportion and therefore incorrectly perceived by a person that is hostile towards their feeling of powerlessness.

The individual must seek to understand the situation better.

Attempts to eradicate this powerlessness are completely or partially misguided and destructive and may upset power structures. The individual is excessively hostile towards the powerlessness and is automatically wrathful.

Some forms of powerlessness are unnatural and destructive and perceived correctly for what they are in form and magnitude.

Action must be taken against this powerlessness, but it must be done in a controlled manner or else the individual is wrathful.

The individual must have courage in facing adversity both natural and unnatural, and must have self-control when trying to perceive and eradicate powerlessness.

As opposed to anger, wrath is absolute. Absoluteness rejects the nuances of any situation and opens up the individual to deterioration if the individual cannot reason, control, or view things with a broad long-term perspective. Wrath is all or nothing in the attempt to eradicate powerlessness. With absoluteness the wrathful individual completely disregards the nuances of power and life, and completely disregards everything external to the self. Everything external to the self is seen as a threat to the individual's power and therefore must be subjugated to the individual's power in retaliation. When an individual is locked into wrathful thinking and acting, the desire to alleviate their suffering becomes insatiable. This leads to extreme behavior.

The insatiability of wrath deteriorates the mind and the individual clashes destructively with the external. The mind that is insatiable for power is a mind of constant suffering with the individual incapable of enjoying life. It is a one-track mind hell bent on destruction. There is no wonder or humor in this mind. The value of life, of both the self and others, plummets. With this plummeting of value with regard to life, the individual is ripe for acting destructively in extreme ways. The insatiability forces the individual to act extremely in the quest for eradicating powerlessness and obtaining power. There is seemingly no other way to handle the situation.

Extreme behavior is behavior that is outside of what is productive and necessary for the preservation of society and life. This extreme behavior comes in many forms, all destructive, which I will discuss later. The wrathful individual lashes out at everything- the external, or even the internal. This individual does not care about the consequences of their actions. Control is discarded, and more or all behaviors are acceptable, no matter how their consequences are played out into the planes of existence. Time ceases to exist. The past is forgotten, the future is irrelevant, the only time is now, the only thing that exists is the individual. Any attempt to regain control over a powerless situation that is not a forceful attempt to quickly remedy the situation is perceived by the individual as dragging themself deeper into weakness, fueling the wrathful individual to seek power faster and more forcibly. After a certain point if the individual perceives that all attempts to gain power are futile, the individual turns to destroying everything that has made them feel the way they do. In the final form of the pursuance of wrath, the destruction of things external to the self and the destruction of the self are intertwined in a complete loss of self-control and rejection of life. If not destruction through wrath, the individual gives up completely on life and destroys themself through depression.

Wrath is on a spectrum, with some level of control and lower magnitude on one end and a complete loss of control and extremeness on the other. Wrath fuels wrath, only control takes a person out of a wrathful state, so a person existing in a low state of wrath will naturally delve deeper and move to the other side of the spectrum. There is a spectrum of wrathfulness in the seeking of extreme power, in the seeking of direct destruction, and in a combination of both. A wrathful individual may easily overlap wrath through the attempt to gain excessive power with wrath by destroying. An individual tends to first seek all of the power they can get and then realize any futility and seek to destroy, but they are intertwined.

Wrath as Power Seeking·

Wrath through power seeking is on a spectrum of destructiveness. Some inconsequential power seeking through wrath is not that destructive, while other extreme forms of wrathful power seeking are highly destructive. Inconsequential power seeking through wrath leads the individual more easily to highly consequential wrathful power seeking.

Wrath does not have to be a violent destructive physical act done in one instance. It can be a long drawn out affair in setting out to control and dominate others over a lifetime. Power and control come in many forms. Examples of the power an individual seeks excessively may be monetary power, political power, or the power to shape people's thoughts and actions with or without them knowing it. The wrathful person seeks extreme monetary power, political power, or influential power because of the control over other people that becomes possible with it. The wrathful person uses these forms of power to obtain more power, and they use the more power to obtain more power. Wrathful people do not use the power they have in influencing people to help those people self-actualize, they only use their power to increase their power even further at the expense of others and to control others for the sake of their own power. The excessive power-seeking in one person is the suffering in another.

Greed is a form of power seeking and insulation from

the world and others. Greed and power seeking both neglect anything external to the individual, whether it is other people or ideas that bring people together, in the attempt to gain power over the given situation. The wrathful greedy person disregards others, exploits others, and hoards their power. This person feels that if they hoard enough power they can gain control over their powerless state of being, yet no matter how much power an individual attains, it is never enough power to compensate for the objective meaninglessness of existence. Hoarding and excessive power-seeking are not the remedy to objective meaninglessness. Due to their ignorance, the wrathful individual still continues their pursuit of power to no end. Living a life of frugality and cooperation aligns a person with the path in attaining happiness in meaninglessness, as you will see later.

Attempting to gain all power leads the individual to power by direct destruction. Power hungry individuals are very likely to be externally and self-destructive individuals in the first place. This is because these two scenarios are of the same nature, wrath. Power-hungry individuals may destroy in order to further their power or they may discard seeking power in control by seeking power in the relinquishing of control and acting in pure destructive wrath. Excessive power-seekers lack a real sense of self, and lack the necessary type of power in order to be happy, so they delve in self-destruction. Wrath always leads to a lower value of life and a lower value of life leads to more wrath. This is where the individual relinquishes all self-control and seeks only to destroy.

Wrath as Destruction:

Wrath is practically synonymous with destruction. An individual may react to a feeling of powerlessness by wildly seeking to destroy. The source and facilitator of all feelings of powerlessness is the framework of existence; human beings are not all-powerful. Something that exacerbates and "creates" the individual's feeling of powerlessness in any situation may not be known, which creates a scenario that is ripe for the individual to lash out in wrath. If an individual has no understanding in how to direct their anger in any concrete direction in order to alleviate the problem, they will devolve into wrath and destroy anything.

The most obvious form of wrath is acute rage involving physical or verbal aggression and destruction. Wrath is an all encompassing feeling and state of being. Violence, murder, outbursts of extreme physical and verbal rage these things come when a person's anger, which has turned into wrath, has reached a pitch. In extreme wrath a rising of tense energy that originates in the front center of the body flows up the spine to the base of the skull. The heart begins to beat at an extreme rate, the nerves of the body fire, and the person becomes extremely on edge. The eyes bulge and look crazed. A person does not have to experience this exact feeling in order to be physically wrathful, as wrathful destruction is wrathful for many reasons spoken about before. Though if an individual is in that state of feeling it is certain that they are in a wrathful state.

Physical violence in itself does not automatically mean an individual is wrathful. The reason for the violence, and state of being and feeling of the individual determine the nature of the violence.

If a person exists in a state of rage and does not act on it they are still on the path of destruction. By constantly being in a state of rage ready to boil over, eventually the person will act on it externally, and if not, it will eat away at the person inside. All internalities have consequences and play out into the mind of the individual and the external world.

Maliciously destroying ideas or societal structures that aim to lift humanity up out of absurdity to create and maintain an enjoyable life is a form of wrath, whether it is destroying those ideas within oneself or among others. When a person gives up and physically destroys, they are at the same time destroying the ideas of self-control and courage in the collective conscious. Ideas that build a society may be targeted in wrath because they represent all that the wrathful person consciously or subconsciously is against or does not care about. The wrathful person seeks disorder and chaos. With no regard for life, the wrathful person seeks to destroy themself, which is the true underlying nature of all wrath; a giving up on life. Wrath is always self-destructive and is the antithesis of building a meaningful and enjoyable existence out of nothingness.

Wrath leads to the cessation of life.

What if society or specific people are currently pushing destruction or pushing destructive tendencies and/or instilling helplessness in yourself or other individuals? Society or other people may act in a destructive manner that may not be directed at a specific person, but may directly or indirectly affect the person nonetheless. Wrath aimed to combat a perceived destructive society may achieve something, but it is always destructive and will be less effective than fighting for a belief with self-control. Wrathful actions always leave irreversible damage to the collective conscious and should be avoided at all costs even if the outcome is the elimination of the original destruction.

An individual that wants to change a destructive system that inflicts powerlessness and suffering must not destroy the system in uncontrollable wrath, the individual must use ANGER to DECONSTRUCT the system to get rid of it and pave the way for a better system.

The individual must have complete understanding of the destructive situation and then take the necessary steps in order to remedy it. This may involve organizing many individuals to combat society-wide problems. Notice the key word being "organizing" as collective organization is a key to building. A lone wolf individual will never be able to personally eradicate societal-wide destructiveness.

These individuals must not organize to act in violence if violence has not been taken against them. Violence, while much braver than doing nothing at all, is the courageous, but messy and destructive way out. The courage needed to take violent action is admirable and is the opposite of choosing to remain content with suffering and weakness, but it is misguided. Controlled and organized violence or physical usurpation of power may be made as a very very last resort if people are subjugated to acute non-physical destructiveness and there is absolutely no hope for any change to be made without violence being needed. If people are pushed too far then organized physical force in order to subdue the destructor may be considered. Organizing people right into physical revolution is not the answer. The true rule of building is to take aggressive non-violent controlled ACTION against destructiveness. Controlled action is the key to building and stopping destruction, doing little or nothing in these areas is the worst of all.

Oppressive societies and individuals that use physical force must be retaliated against with physical force in order preserve the individual and fight against annihilation. Oppressive and destructive individuals who use physical force against a person must be met with physical force if words do not suffice. Pacifism is not the answer in these situations.

The individual or group must always be ready to defend themselves physically, especially if it is highly likely that they will be attacked against physically in the near future due to the defender's actions taken in order to eliminate the powerlessness or not. A bold non-violent statement may entice the destructive entity to retaliate with physical violence. Making a statement and hoping that a destructive entity will simply comply is naïve. The defenders must be ready to push the limits and defend against annihilation.

After saying that individuals must not pursue extreme power, it is very important to say that an individual must seek and have power, not for the sake of gaining more and more power, but for many reasons. The individual must obtain power and knowledge in order to form a strong self. It is on the extreme end of the spectrum where power seeking leads to wrath and self-destruction. You will see why power is needed in the next section.

Building is all about obtaining power in non-destructive ways. A great way to obtain power is to build relationships with other people. With those relationships the individuals have the power to accomplish more, along with the power of enjoyment and solidarity. The ultimate and greatest form of obtaining power is to seek the power of understanding. The truth-seeker and truth-obtainer carries the most power in our meaningless existence.

In the next section I will talk about depression. Depression and wrath are of the same nature; a reaction to powerlessness. They are heavily intertwined in an individual and may be present at the same time if not oscillating.

Depression

The meaninglessness and powerlessness that the individual experiences given the framework of existence can produce a deep reaction of despair in the individual. When a person is faced with the fact that they are not all knowing or not all powerful, one of the ways to cope is to relinquish all power from oneself in hopeless defeat. Faced with too much pointless suffering, the person becomes numb to existence and desires to relinquish all power and responsibility from themself.

Depression is a loss of the will to live. It is a loss of the will to be strong and forge an existence out of nothingness.

To the depressed person, their depression is perceived as thrust upon themselves from the external. The depressed person views themself as an innocent victim, and due to this perceived victimhood they denounce all possibility that the origin of the depression lies within. The individual finds their depression comforting, because it is a state of being void of any responsibility or consequence in which nothing matters. They hide from their suffering in their depression.

This internalized suffering is a reaction to powerlessness. Instead of doing the dance with powerlessness, the individual copes with it by developing a twisted drive to further their powerlessness, hopelessness, and suffering by rationalizing that they are at the base True state of being, and that the individual Deserves this state of being. The external may create powerlessness and suffering in the individual, and the external WILL ALWAYS create suffering in the individual, but the external does not create depression. The individual creates depression. Depression is a choice and it is a choice that does not need to be made, nor should it be made. Depression is a choice to go down the path of least resistance, and without any resistance, the individual will suffer even more. Depression is destructive.

Depression is destructive because it erodes the will to live. All destructive states of being feed upon themselves to create more destructiveness and depression does the same, driving the individual deeper into despair. Without the will to live the outcome is obvious; the individual will cease to exist prematurely without experiencing all that life has to offer, and without contributing to building a collective existence for the future of humanity to experience all that life has to offer. Depression drives humanity into nothingness and is the antithesis of life. If one chooses life, then one must not accept depression or destruction.

Even if the individual does not kill themselves due to their depression, but remains in a lower state of despair, they do just that; exist in a state of despair. Existing in a state of despair leads to a one-dimensional, incomplete, unproductive, wasteful, empty life and this encompasses all aspects of one's being. This is a life that is not worth living, which is why depression feeds upon itself. This state of being resonates into all aspects of the collective conscious and society, dragging humanity down.

Depression is not sadness and sadness is not destructive. Sadness is temporary and is not of an apathetic nature. The extreme nature of the depressed mind is why it is destructive. Depression is extreme apathy and apathy reduces life to nothingness.

Depressed people do not care about anything, which means they do not care about the consequences of their depression. This cycle drives the depressed person down into more extreme apathy. This indifference and numbness makes the individual weak and this feeling of weakness, worthlessness and inferiority creates even more weakness in the individual. Depression creates weakness and only the weak are depressed. Since the individual creates depression, the individual creates weakness in themself and accepts weakness as the Right state of being.

Weakness only hinders the self and only hinders society. The individual may accept weakness as the Right state of being because they feel they are inferior. This inferiority fuels the depression, which may fuel the inferiority. The individual must learn to understand the origin of the inferiority in order to take the necessary steps to overcome it. The origin of inferiority is powerlessness and powerlessness will always exist in a human being no matter how much power they obtain. The individual must strive for power or else they will become completely defeated.

The depressed person feels that it is Right that they are defeated. They feel that being defeated is part of their nature and is part of the nature of humanity. With this defeatism the depressed person loses their animalistic instinct and with that they cease to be sexual beings. This destroys their life further as it is necessary to retain an animalistic and sexual drive in order to retain the will to be strong and masculine or motherly and feminine. This drive also includes the will to be productive for survival and separate from the animalistic component, a drive to build and create a self and society that does not just survive, but thrive. It is up to the individual to recognize that if they choose life, they must be strong and they must build, otherwise their life will crumble. The individual must seek a deeper understanding of existence, and as part of that deeper understanding they must choose to be courageous rather than wallow in depression.

The individual should never let the unchanging base nature of existence, which is meaninglessness and a biological framework, affect themselves in a way that would produce depression. Meaninglessness is unchanging, and things that are unchanging must be danced with and mastered. In the case of meaninglessness mastery is embracing it in pure wonder. Reducing meaninglessness to suffering is useless and destructive.

Although the individual creates depression, external and societal influences may push depression onto the individual. Society is something that is possible to change, but is very difficult to change by one person. If society is destructive and inflicts suffering upon a person, the fact that it is near impossible for one person to change it only exacerbates the suffering. The individual is seemingly powerless, but the individual has the power to change society through their actions and ability to organize with other people. The individual must not let depression overcome themself and drag themselves into further powerlessness and suffering.

It is too simplistic to say that a person should simply not be depressed. Depression must be overcome through shear will by the cultivation of four areas. It takes energy and effort to overcome depression or else the mind will remain in the easily obtained base state of depression forever. The individual must cultivate understanding and power.

It is necessary for the individual to have self-control in order to overcome depression.

It is necessary for the individual to have courage in order to overcome depression.
It is necessary for the individual to have wonder in order to overcome depression.
It is necessary for the individual to have a sense of humor in order to overcome depression.

Madness

If one thinks about the true base nature of existence, which is complete absurdity and meaninglessness without any objective guidance from any higher power, and a free will to think and act in any way one chooses, a mental breakdown can occur. When the mind breaks down the individual finds every behavior imaginable to be acceptable. The chaotic nature of our universe takes hold in the individual and this manifests into mania and a loss of control and function. All social norms and guidelines cease to matter and the individual becomes destructive to all that has been built to allow people to survive and function. This madness displayed to others can spread and lead a social group into a manic breakdown.

To the mad individual, every action is valid. In our day-to-day lives we barely see madness at all, because most people live in blind ignorance to the true nature of existence, incapable of understanding it do to immense social conditioning and a lack of courage to introspect and understand existence. Most that do understand the true base nature of existence can overcome the initial reaction to release control from oneself in order to preserve themselves. Others go mad.

The less formed or structured a mind, the more susceptible that mind is to decay and breakdown. If nothing is built in the first place then there is nothing really to break down. Minds must be formed and structured.

Madness is destructive to the individual because the person whose mind completely deteriorates experiences immense suffering, and the person is no longer able to function or enjoy many components of life. The person may also lash out and inflict suffering onto others.

Madness is agony. The mind is tormented and is at the will of chaos. The individual is no longer in control and this is not a very pleasant feeling. The structure of the mind disintegrates and all that is considered a normal socially conditioned human being is lost. The person that remains is fully human, just not the type of human we interact with day to day. To this person nothing matters and everything humanly possible is justified, so self-destruction follows on top of the self-destruction that occurs with the madness itself.

The most destructive aspect of madness is its destructiveness towards a functioning individual and society. The completely mad person, in a state of extreme turmoil and suffering, cannot function at all. This person does not contribute to the functioning or strengthening of society, and this person may influence the collective conscious and the people around him in creating destructiveness and madness in others. People who are not completely mad do not function very well or at all. To a lesser degree, but still to a degree of destructiveness do these people influence society and the collective conscious.

Because nothing matters to the mad person, they themself don't matter, and the external, with all its people and rules and norms and existencies, is worthless and does not need to be followed or cared for. Depression and wrath can intertwine with madness to form a potently destructive individual with their feelings of powerlessness only directed at everything. Wrath and depression are a form of madness and madness is a form of depression and wrath. The entangling of wrath, depression, and madness drives the individual into a spiral of despair that can only be remedied through de-escalation and regaining control of oneself. That is what the destructive state of being is- the escalation and exacerbation of powerlessness.

As with wrath and depression, society can push the individual to be destructive and go mad. External pressure, and the instilling of hopelessness and powerlessness that goes along with an inability to relieve it, fosters mental breakdowns. In a society full of destructiveness and ignorance, an individual may feel a growing disdain for destructiveness and a pressure to eradicate it if they believe the path of building should be the choice of all humanity. If the pressure builds in the individual, and the individual does not relieve any of this pressure or practice courage and self-control, the individual may break under the weight and go mad.

One of the first things to deteriorate when an individual goes mad is the acceptance of social norms. Strict social norms may cause an individual to snap and go mad. It may be necessary to relax social etiquette a little as a society in order to prevent people from being driven to madness. More relaxation and less pressure in society as whole may help. With meaninglessness and free will, too much constriction can be a problem, but for the same reasons constriction is necessary.

Hedonism

The pursuance of pleasure is something that people can easily fall into given our meaningless existence. Hedonism is easy to follow because it seems logical to pursue things that feel good. In a world where nothing is Logical due to the core absurdity of existence, countless people rely on the thought that pursuing pleasure is Justified because it feels good, and what feels good must be the Right thing to do. This is destructive simplistic thinking.

The "feeling good" aspect of hedonism is short-term physical gratification and does not lead to long lasting content with one's existence. The effects on one's mind and health in pursuing hedonism are deep. Hedonism is escapism and giving up. It is the opposite of facing the challenges of being human. In the end pursuing hedonism leads to deep dissatisfaction and self-destruction. It also leads acutely to the destruction of a civilization.

A person who follows hedonism as a philosophical guideline does not have the courage or self-control to think past the consequences of it's simplicity, nor can they see the destruction it inflicts on their lives and society, because they feel good. Hedonism is destructive because it weakens the mind and narrows the mind. Reducing ones existence to seeking pleasure takes away the individual's ability to appreciate and accomplish other things.

Like all destructive states of being, hedonism is insatiable. Once a hedonistic person desires pleasure and obtains that pleasure, they desire more and more pleasure to satisfy their craving. The biological facilitator of pleasure is dopamine, in which a person needs a larger and larger "fix" to get their "kicks". This insatiability is destructive because the mind of a person who pursues pleasure to no end disintegrates. Sexually the hedonistic person becomes perverted, degenerate and it breaks down their ability to form a bond with another person beyond the use of the other person to quench a sexual need. As a hedonistic person bounces from one sexual partner to another, they are less able to form a meaningful relationship. Later you will see how this plays out in the person's lifetime and how it is expanded to society as a whole. Pursuing sexual deviances and sexual extremes leads to the erosion of society. Hedonism leads to societal decadence. A society in which it is no longer necessary to be strong and disciplined disintegrates into a decadent society and a decadent society will disintegrate until it becomes necessary to discard hedonism in order to survive or else it will fall into societal collapse- or even worse- remain stagnate in a hell of decadence.

Hedonists seek instant gratification, and only gratification, and with this they don't have the discipline to accomplish anything. Reducing one's existence to the pursuit of pleasure reduces one's mind to a simplistic undisciplined slop. The person neglects other needs and must rely on other strong people to help them accomplish things.

A lot of times the pursuit of pleasure leads to the direct result of something acutely destructive happening on top of the slow destruction the mind. People may overdose on drugs. People may destroy their bodies with gluttony. These people become either useless or dead.

In the end hedonists are self-destructive because they create a life that is not worth living. There is no wonder in the hedonists mind. At the core of the hedonistic person is a person that is really depressed, because pleasure does not facilitate self-actualization, a connection with the universe, or any connection with others.

Although the pursuance of hedonism is destructive, it is good to seek some pleasure as part of experiencing and enjoying life and to act as a pressure valve. Pursuing some pleasure is not only "not destructive"; it is absolutely necessary and beneficial to pursue some pleasure. The complete deprivation of all pleasure is destructive. By denying oneself from all pleasure the person only fuels the deep down desire to pursue pleasure until this pressure builds up and manifests into the person rejecting their choice of denial and swinging to the other extreme end of the spectrum into the complete pursuance of hedonism and destruction.

This is not a go ahead to do whatever you want as a release of the pressure valve. A small component of ones life should be seeking pleasure, control and discipline are highly important. And by only pursuing "some" pleasure I don't only mean the magnitude, I mean only certain avenues of pleasure. Certain avenues of pleasure should not be pursued at all due to their far-reaching negative consequences and the extent one delves into an area of pleasure should be greatly restricted. The complete denial of sexual urges is bad, but these sexual urges must be taken care of in a healthy way. Seeking to gratify sexual urges through numerous sex partners, porn, or sexual deviancy should be discarded.

Ignorance

The root of all destruction is ignorance. To be a builder, one must be a truth-seeker. If one chooses life, one must choose to be a truth-seeker.

A person will stay in a state of complete ignorance if they do not take the first step in living and question their existence. The first step in living is gaining some control over the mind. The mind is the fusion of the external with the internal and will stray in any way the external directs it if not for a disciplined internal self. The undisciplined and unfocused person remains complacent and accepts the reality they are initially presented with as True. This person is distracted by all unnecessary and useless information. There must be a step in controlling and honing the mind to certain avenues of thought.

The first step in controlling the mind to begin on the path out of ignorance is to cultivate wonder- to develop a curiosity of why things are and an awareness and awe of the unknown. One must analyze and question their existence and everything within existence. One must introspect, and introspect a level deeper by analyzing the introspection, and introspect a further level by analyzing the analysis of the introspection. In order to begin on the path out of ignorance a person must question their existence and come to the frightful initial realization that they actually act and exist with free will in a meaningless existence. This is when a person begins living- when they know they exist. A person who lives in blind ignorance does not know they exist. A person cannot build or create if they lack consciousness and awareness.

A person remains in ignorance due to indifference and fear. One must have a mixture of wonder and courage in order to desire to take the first step into the unknown. The acute powerlessness one subconsciously feels as they venture into the unknown prevents the person from breaking free. Left to its devices, the mind will keep a person in ignorance to preserve itself because it believes that an acute feeling of powerlessness may destroy the mind and the individual. One must have the courage to supersede the impulse of self-preservation in order to seek truth because in the end this self-preservation is not preservation at all- it is stagnation and destruction.

After the initial step is made to leave ignorance, one may stagnate and be unable to drive deeper. In order to drive oneself deeper into understanding and break free from the shackles of ignorance, one must have wonder. But when one opens up their mind to wonder and goes deeper they experience great suffering, confusion, and chaos. This is where control and courage are vital, as a tremendous resistance to pursue deeper occurs. Control is also needed to not allow the mind to destroy itself in letting in too much of the meaninglessness and chaos of existence.

Wonder remains as the most important aspect. The root of all understanding is wonder. The root of all creation is wonder because creation follows after one reaches the understanding of the duality of human nature.

Ignorance is destructive because it is a state of unnecessary powerlessness and incompleteness. It takes a keen, attentive, and focused path to cultivate power, build, and create an enjoyable and complete life that is worth living and that strengthens society. Without the power of understanding, the ignorant person does not have any control and makes decisions that are destructive, or doesn't make the necessary right decisions in order to build. Ignorance is a lack of control. Ignorance pushes humanity in any direction because there is no understanding of the nature of existence. By cultivating understanding, the individual increases their power in making the right decisions. These right and wrong decisions are a matter of life and death. Yet an individual or society may operate in ignorance and they will continue on because an ignorant person or society are insulated from the meaninglessness of existence, and because some right decisions may unconsciously be made. In the long term ignorance's stagnation and incorrectness leads to absolute destruction.

Stagnation is the antithesis of continual building and understanding. Stagnation is deterioration. A stagnate and directionless humanity flounders in confusion. Being directionless means that there is no common understanding of what it takes to build, nor any understanding of the necessity to build and maintain. Degeneracy flourishes in stagnation as individuals delve into hedonism and deviancy. Life is about constantly moving, striving, and reaching. If an individual stagnates they will perish. If a species stagnates it will perish.

Ignorance is apathy and indifference. The consequences of indifference are a lack of focused attention in necessary building or curbing of destructiveness, and a shallow, hollow, incomplete, and wasteful life. The fool's life is shallow and wasteful. It is a choice to deny the wonders of the world. But an individual should not and cannot be forced to learn about the world. Fear and destruction should not be the motivating factor in pushing a person to seek understanding. An interest in the world creates an enjoyable life. Philosophy is the love of wisdom and the love of wisdom is the love of life. It is not necessarily the consequences that should motivate a person, but what they gain in wonder, understanding, and enjoyment. A student should not be motivated to learn because of the fear of being scolded for getting bad grades, but should be motivated by their own interest in learning.

Life is what you create it to be. Awareness and consciousness are not given, they must be forged, and any human being that has the capacity to create awareness within themselves must take advantage of it. A person who does not cultivate awareness will exist with what they created- a destructive worthless life of shallowness and incompleteness, and this resonates into every action and instance of their existence.

Life is full of distraction and the ignorant person is heavily distracted. The individual is distracted away from forging a path of understanding. A cultivation of an instinctive knowing of what is essential over nonessential in order to forge a path of understanding is needed. Although there are endless unique paths to understanding, they all have one thing in common; a direct focus in retaining what is essential and shaving off all uselessness and wrongness. The path to understanding is not simple and direct though. There must be countless discardations of what was once considered useful and true information that is revealed to be incorrect. The ability to recognize one's incorrectness and quickly discard it for superior understanding is what separates a builder from someone who wallows in ignorance and destructiveness.

A society that creates ignorance is destructive. People who maliciously try to make and keep other people ignorant for control and their own benefit are extremely destructive. The motive of people who purposely dumb others down is never a benevolent attempt to "guide" people and keep these people away from harming themselves. The motive is almost always excessive greed, power-seeking, or a twisted amusement. People who are extremely wrathful in power-seeking and hoarding power may desire to subject people to ignorance in order to control them and maintain and further their position of power. What an existence. But ignorance largely festers in society through face to face interactions between people in everyday life. Social etiquette, or the allowance of saying one thing or the other in any given situation, is the facilitator of ignorance. If one person is in a position of higher understanding and another person makes a remark that is incorrect, it is likely that the person who knows more will just go along with the other in order to not upset anyone. Especially in a situation where people interacting create a social atmosphere where it is unacceptable to venture into political incorrectness does the truth and reality of the situation, especially if it is politically incorrect, never see the light of day and reach other people's consciousnesses. A person of higher understanding must be firm and stand his ground, yet be tactical and gracious in getting his point across. A person who is ridiculed or thrown out into the open of their own ignorance will not be in a position of acceptance and building upon the ideas presented, and the new ideas may greatly upset their mental order if they are not mentally ready for them.

The Foundations for Exploration and Building

Self-Control

Free will allows for the individual to think, feel and act in any way. As we have seen a lot of these ways are destructive to the creation and preservation of a life worth living. This means that self-control is the greatest tool in the creation of a strong individual and society.

The individual may allow themself to be consumed by the meaninglessness of the void and be drawn to all five forms of destruction. It takes understanding and discipline in order to pull oneself out of the pit of infinity where the mind is lost and cannot form subjective structure. The mind craves its own destruction. The self must supersede all of the ways the mind is driven toward destruction through self-control.

You are alive. It is important to realize this from time to time, or all of the time to a certain extent. When you know you are alive you know that you are creating your existence continuously and always. Your level of consciousness determines how strongly you shape your mind and existence. Rather than being provided with an existence only from the external and "living" in a slumber, the builder recognizes that they are alive, faces the consequences of reaching this understanding, and takes control over their mind and life, influencing their own mind with an overarching self that is focused. That is the importance of self-control, to focus and connect one's thoughts.

In order to reach higher understandings of existence, and to reach contentment, it takes discipline. Paths must be taken and experiences must be had and shaped. It takes self-control to reach truth, and with that truth one has the opportunity to have more control and power over their life. Without this honing self-control of the mind, the individual will not develop understanding quickly.

Discipline is not only used for the direct action of truth-seeking, it should be practiced in all areas of life and in daily life. External influence must be met with controlled reaction and action. All actions influence one's life and all actions influence the collective conscious. The seemingly insignificant instances in one's life are important.

It takes discipline to maintain the mind and it takes discipline to preserve and strengthen the body. The mind and the body are one unit. They are not separate. It is important to take care of one's body and in doing so it disciplines and strengthens the mind. Taking care of the body should not be done in the extreme however. It is destructive to be overly concerned with the look of one's body, and it is destructive to pursue extreme healthiness, because extreme healthiness does not matter and it is too much focus in one area of one's life. For men in the cultivation of strength it should not be taken to the extreme because it focuses too much in one area of one's life. Men who take the cultivation of strength and physical appearance to the extreme have a deeper insecurity in their masculinity.

Self-control must be made in frugality. Without frugality one is wasteful and one seeks too much power. A Spartan-like way of living benefits all other areas of one's life and keeps a person focused, collected, and strong.

Self-control does not mean existing in a state of passivity. Self-control does not mean that a person should not act on the infliction of powerlessness and suffering directed towards them. A person should act in a controlled and thought-out manner that will be the most effective and least destructive way of remedying the situation.

Self-control is absolutely necessary, but it does not have to be excessively monitored or practiced, otherwise you'll lose your goddam mind. A person must balance strict command with going with the flow. Going with the flow may not always be losing control, but gaining it, because the consequences of grating against the flow in certain situations may lead to break down or error. Extreme restriction of the self leads to self-destruction. The human mind is not equipped to handle an overload of constriction. One must be aware of the mind's nature and needs, and recognize that allowing the mind the freedom to wander is essential. That is how I personally operate. I allow my mind to wander and follow avenues of thought while shaping the thoughts and naturally intervening when appropriate. All of this comes naturally with time, and over time an individual gracefully exists with the understanding that they are alive and are responsible for shaping their existence. An overly sensitive and obsessive person must learn to be cool.

An individual must especially recognize the things that one can change and the things that one cannot change. Reaching the understanding that the situation is one that is impossible to change is the first step. Going from there it takes nuance if the unchangeable situation is causing suffering. Influencing one's own perspective surrounding the unchangeable situation instead of trying to change the situation itself is needed. Saying that one must cultivate an acceptance of the situation and everything will be fine is far too simplistic. Navigating the situation may involve simply not thinking about it if it causes too much suffering. Constantly thinking about an unchangeable and horrible situation drags down and pins the individual into a destructive mindset. A masterful builder recognizes what must be thought about and what must not and moves on, for the sake of control and strength.

In challenging times, displaying weakness creates more weakness in oneself. It is wise to remain in control and show no weakness, unless the subtle controlled showing of weakness is appropriate and brings more power (not in a manipulative sense).

Courage

The nature of courage is the nature of building.

You will face immense suffering, adversity, and absurdity, which are all forms of powerlessness, on your journey. If you do not face these challenges with an unwavering courage, they will destroy you.

The weak are swept away and destroyed when faced with powerlessness, but the courageous know how to live with and channel powerlessness, and if necessary, attack it. An individual may be destroyed by an adversary, but if he acted courageously, he was never destructive and the nature of his being will live on in others. Only the weak believe that it is foolish to be courageous, because they do not see its power.

You must have courage to seek truth. Only through the seeking of truth does the individual begin to live. Therefore in order to begin to live, one must have courage. With the understanding of certain truths, it opens up great suffering. One must have resilience and resolve in driving deeper through despair in order to reach understanding and nirvana. Nirvana is the acceptance of life as worth it, and the understanding that the path of building is the path one must take. You must have courage to live by your truths.

The unknown will always be a part of existence. Absurdity will always be a part of existence. Powerlessness will always be a part of existence. Our biological needs will always be a part of existence. It takes courage to face these challenges.

It takes courage to recognize things that you can change, and recognize things that you cannot change. It then takes courage to deal with the consequences of the unchanging. One may be powerless due to the unchanging, but there is power in understanding it. The greatest power of all is understanding.

It takes courage to exist in a society of destructiveness. It takes courage to try and contribute to and build a society that is destructive. A society of destructiveness may be directly destroying an individual, or others may be destroying the individual. It takes courage to restrain oneself from acting in wrath, and also to retaliate in controlled action. A society of destructiveness may instill hopelessness in the individual because the individual may feel helpless and powerless in their capability in influencing a dire situation at large. It is necessary to have hope in order to have courage. Courage implies that there is an adversity that can be overcome, so there must be a hope to achieve the overcoming. A society that instills helplessness and hopelessness is dangerous because it erodes the courage to keep on trying.

One must have determination in life and a determination to be on the path of building.

Wonder

Wonder is the most important foundation in exploration, understanding, and building.

Life becomes not worth living if it loses its mysteriousness in the eyes of the individual. We are ingrained with a sense of wonder from birth, but may ignore and "lose" this feeling with time. Other things, or everything, get in the way of the individual in feeling a sense of wonder. Yet life will always be a dream at its core and the individual must realize this. Perceiving the world with wonder intertwines the individual with the universe, and curiosity sustains life, because life is not worth living if everything is known. We must strive for all-knowledge but accept and enjoy our sense of wonder that arises in being a human being, ignorant of life's unanswerable questions.

The powerlessness that comes with meaninglessness creates all of the suffering in the world, but from the same meaninglessness we have wonder, which makes life worth living.

This entire essay may seem like I have set out to put humanity into a box, restrict it, and make it submit to a rigid set of rules, but I believe the exact opposite is true. With my organization of thought I believe I am not restricting humanity, but providing a foundation for humanity to explode off of into freedom and exploration. With knowledge comes freedom from the servitude of ignorance.

With wonder comes a passion for life. The individual is infused with the spirit of exploration and life resembles an adventure rather than a burden. A human being is meant to explore. It is in our nature.

Exploration creates excitement. It implies continual and never ending newness, which is what our universe has provided for us. Life is constantly changing, never stopping, and is never capable of being understood. Children perceive the world with complete wonder, and we are always children of the universe.

I place humanity as the creators of our own existence and with this it may seem that any concept of a God has been discarded. My philosophy does not discard a God, but rather enhances the possibility of there being higher powers. If there are higher powers, I believe these higher powers may have helped create us, but do not have sway over our actions and lives like any conventional God. Free will, and free creation exist. I believe these higher powers must be beings that wonder just as we do. These beings may exist under the same pretenses as our duality of human nature. The higher powers may have helped create us in order for us to exist under these identical pretenses. Regardless of anything, humanity must always consider the possibility of powers beyond our understanding, just as we consider and know that there is knowledge beyond our understanding.

Sense of humor

With humor, absurdity is contentment.

Humor is an important and effective defense mechanism if absurdity is causing suffering in someone, and you must have a sense of humor to curb the destructiveness that comes with a life that is too serious, mundane and full of pressure. But these statements reduce humor to only a tool when it is far more than that.

Humor is becoming one with the universe and becoming one with one another.

Confusion and tension become ease, a release of relief, and a relish in joy due to the feeling of pressure being lifted and replaced with understanding and connection.

I'm not telling you to "use" humor. I'm telling you to not forget about it.
I'm not telling you how to develop a sense of humor, but if I did I would say to embrace the absurd.

Our universe is absurd, laugh it up. Instances of absurdity in our lives, in which illogicalness, irrationality and ridiculousness are brought into the forefront remind us of this. Humor is the understanding of absurdity and the mastery of it. Absurdity should not be denied or battled, it should be danced with.

When life becomes too serious the individual begins to become destructive because a mundane life full of pressure is not worth living. When things get too serious the person starts to worry, may become depressed, and will suffer. The seriousness may be a sense of pressure, but it may also involve a life that is not interesting whatsoever. Something that is uninteresting may involve pressure along with being dull as well. Uninteresting implies a lack of any stimuli. Humor alleviates this sense of pressure and makes things interesting. Humor implies something occurring out of normalness.

Too much pressure creates wrath, depression, madness, and turns people to hedonism.

Humor is simply a prime component in enjoying life.

With too much humor, one becomes complacent, weak, and dismissive in taking action against destructiveness or in taking action in building. Part of life is simply having the courage to deal with the mundane parts of life and not escaping from them by making them seem unnecessary and pointless if they require attention. Part of life is having the courage to face destructiveness in oneself and society head on through action and not allow for its existence and let it grow by laughing it off all of the time. Although a completely destructive society may need to be laughed at a little in order to preserve one's sanity. Life is absurd.

Section 3: Power, Biology and Society

Maintaining a strong society is vital for the success of the human race.

Society is an application of the collective conscious for the organization of individuals.

Society has created beings that are different and more than just animals, but we still retain an underlying animalistic nature.

Society is full of individuals that interact with one another. Each of these individuals must have a degree of autonomy and individual power in order to be on the path of building, but as one individual gains more power, others may lose it, and can fall into destructiveness through wrath and especially despair. Society provides guidelines for social interactions and the allocation of power.

Considering these two important components of human nature (Underlying Animal/ Underlying Power) in relation to society:

1. A strong society is based in balancing the pursuance of our biological nature completely and the rejection of our biological nature.
2. A strong society is based in balancing the desire to obtain all power and the desire to relinquish all power from ourselves.

These are the Biological-Artificial Spectrum and the Power Spectrum.

In order to apply the two spectrums to determine the destructiveness or constructiveness of a society, we have to first look at whether society is necessary at all. Is it destructive to not have a society?

No Society

Without others, the individual mind deteriorates, no relationships are formed and life is simply not worth living. In groups of people without a structured society, people revert to power-seeking and animalistic behavior. To rise above our animalistic nature a society takes the collective conscious of a group of people and organizes it to provide accepted knowledge to build off of. It then creates guidance based on that accepted knowledge and cooperation may be formed between people. Under this organization of the collective conscious, relationships are formed between people and strong relationships make life worth living. Without meaningful social interaction, the individual feels completely alone. The individual is not connected to others and is not connected to humanity as a whole. The isolation and loneliness leads the individual to hopeless despair.

The power of strong relationships is involved in everything from the enjoyment of a one on one exchange of words, to the creation of a family, to the ability to accomplish tasks that allow people to decrease the amount of time spent directly on survival. This increases survival rates and decreases the amount of suffering related to a life solely devoted to survival and not experiencing the range of thought and emotion that makes surviving worth it. Other people are not needed for simply creating a mind and society that functions:

> At the core of human existence, other people make life worth living. The social interactions that one experiences over the course of their lifetime are the reason why life has value. Without unity you have despair, destruction, and the extinction of the human race.

Destructive Societal Imbalance:
Too Much Power Seeking and Animalistic Behavior

A societal structure that fosters and allows for too much animalistic behavior or power-seeking behavior is destructive. A society comprised of power-hungry and animalistic people is destructive.

A society full of power-hungry individuals wastes an enormous amount of energy on conflict as opposed to cooperation, understanding, and building. Conflict will always and should always exist, but too much conflict only drags humanity down. Individuals must seek power to form a strong self, but must not seek an excessive amount. As said in the section above on wrath, excessive power seekers desire power for the sake of power in order to dominate others and benefit themselves. Excessive power seekers only care about themselves, which means they have no problem in destroying others to further their own power.

Excessive animalistic behavior means selfishness, an excessive drive to pursue sex, a drive for unnecessary violence, an antagonistic mentality, and a survival of the fittest mentality. Animalistic behavior is very similar to excessive power-seeking behavior, but there is a distinction in that animalistic behavior is more of an unconscious base desire and bodily drive (like an animal) rather than power-seeking which may involve a broader scope and higher thinking. The two are heavily intertwined though.

A society comprised of power-seeking people polarizes the population, leaving a small percentage with all the power, and the rest powerless, helpless, weakened, hopeless, and defeated. The quality of life is greatly diminished for the vast percentage of the population, the productivity of the society is greatly diminished, and the lives of those who reach the top of the power pyramid are shallow, unfulfilled, and full of self-destructive tendencies that reduce the quality of their life. The reason why a society that is characterized by power-hungry and animalistic behavior becomes polarized is because the people that gain power weaken those they obtain power over. The power that is obtained by one person does not necessarily have to be taken from another person, but if it is, it means the person that it was taken from becomes weaker. The powerful become more powerful, and the weaker become even weaker until social or individual unrest reaches a breaking point and an attempt to balance power occurs, or the weak are completely destroyed. Existing in unrest creates a hotbed for a destructive state of being for an individual or society.

Social unrest is terrible for the productivity of a society. Conflict is waste. Conflict divides people and lone individuals that scrap at one another for their share do not accomplish as much as a solid unit of people working together focused on their task. You cannot forget that the enjoyment of company is what makes life worth living. Individuals set on destroying each other miss out on the power of the human bond.

A strong constructive individual and constructive society encourages weak individuals to pursue and create strength and creates environments for the growth of strength. The more strong the better. It is necessary for society to strive to make all individuals strong in order for the society to be building and actualizing. A polarized society is always destructive because it is not striving for the actualization of all of its potential.

Animalistic people are unnecessarily violent, and unnecessary violence destroys all involved. In the animal kingdom it is survival of the fittest and violence and fighting are the norm. In the creation of social hierarchies animals of the same kind are violent towards one another yet in this situation they delay serious conflict until it is absolutely necessary for their preservation. It is not necessary for human beings to resort to violence in constructing social hierarchies unless they are being destructive. Animals fight and kill one another because they are incapable of understanding anything outside of their own biological self-interest in survival.

Human beings that are overly aggressive and violent to others are like simple-minded animals that only have the capability of thinking for their selfish interests. What separates humanity from pure animalism is our ability to cooperate. A society full of people that act like simple-minded violent animals is not a strong society.

Animalistic nature is not limited to violence- it applies to sexuality. A society comprised of people that follow a completely animalistic sexual nature is destructive. The consequences of following this nature are far-reaching. A hedonistic nature and an animalistic sexual nature can be intertwined and this will be discussed later.

Complete animalistic sexual behavior in men is characterized by the pursuance of having sex with many women with disregard for choosing a single mate to create a family with.

Complete animalistic sexual behavior in women is characterized by the pursuance of a man or many men for only their high sexual prowess with disregard for the creation of a strong family due to:
A. The desire for the woman to put off raising a family in this pursuit, which also contributes to a long-term negative effect in the creation of a family in section C.
B. The unlikelihood that a man with high sexual prowess will settle down and raise a child with the particular woman given the fact that he has many other options and may be animalistic himself.
C. The elimination of the possibility of raising a strong family with a man who has less sexual prowess than any man the woman has had sex with before. The reason for this is that a woman will only remain subservient and desire to be with the person who is the top alpha male in her sexual past. The woman is subservient to the feelings and pleasure that the alpha male gave her. A man who remains in a relationship with a woman in which he has no possibility for becoming the top alpha male in her sexual history is a beta and therefore weaker and inferior to the actual alpha male from the perspective of the woman and her feelings. If the woman

disregards her sexual hierarchy and starts a family with a beta male, the partnership is doomed to be weak and they will fail in remaining together and fail to create strong offspring. The woman may have chosen the beta for his provider status because of her inability to hold down an alpha male. The beta is a provider of both monetary and emotional support for the woman. The woman is the dominant person in the relationship with the beta male because she holds the locus of the power in the relationship- her sexual feelings and needs that are not being met.

In a society that heavily leans on the animalistic side, the vast majority of the male population does not have a stake in society because they are not having sex, and they are not reproducing. The animalistic men have sex with many women that range on the sexual value scale from high to low value. The animalistic women only choose to have sex with top men, even though they may be of a lesser sexual value and risk being discarded, or they desire to move from top male to top male. As you can see the people that are having sex are only top men and women. Men that are not top men, which may be the bottom 90 or 80 percent of men in the population, are not having sex or are barely having sex with women that are well below the women of equal sexual value that these men would normally be having sex with if society was not comprised of animalistic men and women. Men and women of equal sexual value would pair and everyone would be having sex and forming relationships no matter what their sexual value is. Animalistic women may eventually decide to settle down with lesser value men than they have experienced before, and these men will have some sex, but to say that those pathetic instances of manipulative pity sex count as healthy is delusional and wrong. It is important for a society that everyone, especially men, is having consistent healthy sex and this plays out later in the formation of a strong family.

The number of sexual partners in a woman's past matters. The higher the partner count, the more likely that one of her previous partners was of greater sexual value than her current partner if in a relationship. High partner counts are also correlated with an animalistic woman who seeks men that are of much greater sexual value than herself. The effects on a man in being in a relationship with a woman who has had sex with someone in her past of greater sexual value are tremendous and ruinous. The woman has experienced someone of greater value and expects that same value or better in the future- it is in her nature to feel this way. If not fulfilled, the woman will not appreciate her man, develop a growing resentment and disrespect towards him, and be depressed. The man will feel inferior and be depressed and this is the important aspect. The relationship should be broken by either side as a mismatch, but if not, destruction follows. The higher the sex count in women, the higher the stakes are for these women to find a suitable man, and the less likely men of lower sexual value will find a women of the same sexual value that has not had sex with someone of higher sexual value. It is important for women to have respect for the truth and therefore have respect for themselves, other men, and the betterment of society. If women do not have a respect for the truth I have laid out above, then they are ignorant or wrathful. If men do not have a respect for the necessary curbing of being animalistic, then they are ignorant or wrathful.

The men of lower sexual value (which may be 80 to 90 or even 99 percent of the total male population depending on how animalistic or hedonistic the women in the population are) that are not having sex in the animalistic society revert to activities that attempt to fill the sexual void, but this in turn only weakens the man even further and may completely destroy the man. Without consistent sex, which is least destructive if in a consistent long-term relationship, it is easy for masculinity in men to decline and it is replaced with depression, weakness and the man may even start to develop femininity. Men who are not having sex do not have a stake in society, and if they did, their diminished masculinity, depression and weakness do not build society to its greatest potential. A man who is not having sex not only loses his care for building society, he does not care for life in general. The man is not only missing out on sex, he is missing out on one

44

of the greatest and most important things that makes
worth living- the loving companionship of a person of t..
opposite sex. This is a life that is not worth living, leading
destruction.

The large percentage of men are constantly
bombarded with sexual women, but are denied access to sex.
The denial of sex creates wrath and depression. In order to be
happy and in order to retain a healthy level of animalistic
nature, men need a sexual outlet, but if there are no women
that want to be in relationships the man's only choices are to
experience a sexual outlet by becoming highly animalistic and
pursuing casual sex, rape, or relinquishing power and
animalistic nature through masturbation. Even though
masturbation is a sexual outlet, it is an unhealthy one that
only weakens the man and makes him more frustrated and
unsatisfied.

The denial of sex is one of the worst sufferings a man
can experience. This is part of why women should dress
modest. Dressing immodest attracts sexual attention.
Immodest dress is defined as wearing clothes that showcase
the body of the woman through either exposure or tightness.
Women that dress immodestly in public are attracting sexual
attention from other men and this is bad for many reasons.
Whether she is in a relationship or single, this sexual
attraction causes the men viewing her to desire to have sex
with her. This desire is 99.9999999999% likely to not be
gratified in every instance a man looks at the woman. This
rising of desire and denial of fulfillment creates a great
negative physiological and mental effect on the man. If the
man does not feel a desire to have sex with the sexually
attractive woman showcasing her sexuality, he is no longer a
man and this is bad. With the sexual liberation of women,
women only choose to have sex with the very top percentage
of men. This exacerbates the mental destruction of the rest of
men because they hopelessly realize they will never have sex
with women who are even on their same level and realize that
these women are only choosing top tier men. If she is a
relationship the man in the relationship is a cuck and/or a

ys/allows the showcasing of his woman. He
ise he contributes to the situation above. If
modestly and in a relationship, she is
on from other men thus cucking the man in
ecause the immodest dress is signaling she is
ugh attention from her man and is seeking
n other men. She may consciously or
..nt a better man and may act on the
attention she gains by dressing immodestly and leave her man
for another.

Feminism creates an imbalance in the power structure
between men and women. Feminism aims to put all power
into the hands of women at the expense of men. When men
lose certain power there are consequences, and consequences
for women in the end as well. Feminism ruins men and ruins
women.

The equality that feminism in this age proposes is not
equality at all; it is plain usurpation and excessive power-
seeking. A society in which women seek and obtain more
power than men is completely destructive. Men must always
remain dominant over women in certain areas of life, if not
men are submissive to women and will cease to be masculine
or "men". There is no magical land of equality in these certain
areas of life. Men must remain dominant, women must have
power, strength, and stability in femininity, submissiveness,
and grace in these areas for the sake of all humanity.

The equality (which isn't even aimed to be equality but rather
power usurpation and allocation for more power for women
than men) that feminism pushes should be analyzed in two
ways:
1. Are the sexes really equal in the area of focus?
2. Should women be made equal in the area of focus?

Feminists push for women to be accepted as equal in
masculine areas of focus, or deserving of the allowance to
participate in these masculine areas of focus even though they
may be inferior.

46

Any area of focus with power being granted to women that undermines the necessary strength of the area of focus should not allow women to be granted the power.

Any area of focus with power being granted to women that destroys male cohesion and bonding should not allow women to be granted the power.

Any area of focus with power being granted to women that masculinizes women or feminizes men should not allow women to be granted the power.

The undermining of necessary strength in an area of focus for the sake of adding women is destructive. Simple as that.

Male cohesion and bonding is a very important thing that can be easily overlooked. Men need to be able to come together and discuss life without the disturbance of women, men need to enjoy each other's company, and men even need to achieve things with other men in solidarity. It is important that masculine pursuits remain masculine, as opposed to being undermined with femininity, and remain something that men can come together for as an outlet to express their masculinity and bond with other men. If the area of focus demands strength and solidarity and results, male cohesion can be something that is necessary to meet those demands as opposed to women undermining the group simply by existing in the group, even if on paper the woman is technically qualified.

Feminists push for women to be put into positions of economic power even though these very positions destroy women and men. Notice how I said "put" into positions, rather than obtaining these positions by merit. Feminists argue for the allocation of power to women even if they lack the merit to earn the power. They want women to be on the same plane as men even if they are not of the same qualifications and skill. Even if these women are of the same skill, it is destructive for them to be in these positions because they masculinize the women, feminize the men, and destroy male cohesion and bonding the same way a man would disturb the female cohesion in heavily woman dominated field.

The masculinization of women is destructive. Feminism is women desiring to be like men, and this is disastrous. Man and woman are not of the same nature and should not be pushed to become of the same nature. I will speak more on the destructiveness of masculinity in women and femininity in men later, but I will say this now: Men are not and should not be attracted to dominant power-seeking women. Dominant women expect men to "handle" their dominant behavior. Dominant women expect to pair with the best men and expect to mate with men who are even more dominant than them, but the top men who are more dominant do not want to bother with these women. Instead these women do not pair at all or pair with weaker men. These weaker men have to settle with these dominant women because they have no other options, do not want to be alone, and are ignorant. The combination of a dominant woman and beta man is a disaster.

As women entire the same fields as men, they naturally feminize the field and the men within it. The office becomes a center of gossip. Entire industries become dominated by women and force men to submit to feminization or be ostracized. The field and society might have greatly benefited from the original base masculine nature to begin with. Men become feminized and become unhappy, broken, and lose the edge of being a man, and everyone suffers for it. On top of the feminization that comes with being equals with women in the workplace, the feminization and destruction of man is far worse when men are in a position of subordinance and subservience to women on a consistent basis. This is a serious matter that I will go into later in more depth. Women may also disrupt a masculine work environment. Drama becomes more prevalent, and women add an unnecessary sexual component to the workplace. Of course not every workplace must be segregated, but some fields are dragged down by allowing women to enter for these reasons.

Women in the workplace also provides women with more sexual opportunities, and sexual liberation is exactly

48

what feminists desire. Feminists push for women's sexual liberation because they want more power. This power comes in the form of unrestricted freedom and the expectation that there should be no consequences for this unrestricted freedom. This sexual liberation and power comes at the expense of society. Society is done for with the sexual liberation of women.

One of the powers that feminists of the past pushed for was women's voting rights. The issue was if women had the "right" to vote, or if they were of equal intelligence and understanding of what it takes to build and run a society rather than be destructively ignorant. If women did not have the exact same understanding of reality, would theirs be different but equally valuable and important for all? Who's to say that allowing women to vote those years ago was the right choice given their track record? Have women proved to have a superior or equal grasp of society as men? There is still belief today that allowing women to vote was a grand mistake for the preservation of society because their votes tend to undermine the strength and structure of a society along with undermining masculinity. The real question is if women have an undeniably different collective mental make up compared to men. The different mental makeup would be due to biology and worldly experience. A difference may partly be due to the fact that women do not experience the world as men, nor could it be said that they have the same ability to comprehend the life of men compared to the ability of men to comprehend the life of a woman. The fact remains that men were and should continue to be the true primary builders and maintainers of society in masculine areas of focus. It would be great if women could understand what comes with being the true builders and maintainers in these areas of focus, but they would cease to be women if they developed the ability to be one of these builders and maintainers. Men do not completely understand what it is like to be a woman, but being a builder and maintainer of society allows men to have the comprehension of what Not being one of these builders or maintainers is like.

Given the nature and history of women, it may be clear that women today do not understand power and are irresponsible when given power. Women tend to abuse their power when given the slightest amount of it. The reason why they take advantage of all granted power may be because they exist as beings of less physical power than men, and they desire to make up for this by obtaining and pushing the limit in other forms of power. With the widespread notion that women should not be retaliated against physically by men, problems can arise if women push the limit in obtaining power over men without consequence- both in the fact that men in this situation exist in a state of suffering, and in the fact that they may eventually act on this suffering in the form of wrath directed at the woman, themselves, or society.

Feminism is the clueless or malicious dissemination of power incorrectly to women.

There is an imbalance in the power spectrum when power is disseminated cluelessly or maliciously wrong.

Those who are in power that cluelessly or maliciously disseminate power to those that do not deserve the power are destructive. Giving power to those who have not earned it weakens those individuals and weakens those that actually do deserve power. The disseminator may be weakened by the clueless dissemination, or may gain strength through malicious dissemination by subjecting the more capable in overthrowing to powerlessness in favor of giving their deserving power to those that will squander it.

There is an imbalance in the power spectrum when people are ignorant of the nature of power. Cluelessly giving power to those that will squander it affects everyone negatively. A person must cultivate strength themself, not be totally reliant on others. If a person is given something that they have not earned, they only become weaker and drag down the rest of society with them. The power is squandered.

Those who are given power are far more likely to abuse the power and overstep their bounds. The weak may desire to strong-arm the formerly more powerful others who deserve that power and this leads to disaster. The malicious weak do not understand the nature of power and the concept of the usurpation of power. When power is usurped, it leaves wrath in its wake. When the weak wield their power and manipulate the truly strong, wrath boils. Revolt is imminent. Revolt is the right thing to do in this case, but due to the nature of the situation it is highly likely to come in the form of wrath. A balancing of the power spectrum is hopeful regardless of the form of revolt, yet excessive destruction should always be minimized. If there is no revolt, then the individuals subjected to unnecessary powerlessness are highly likely to become destroyed in depression. In today's society, due to the eradication of masculinity on all fronts and constriction, ridicule, and attack on all forms of male disapproval, it is extremely likely that men who have had power usurped become depressed and fade into oblivion, or if they possess masculinity, a lashing out in wrath due to the eradication of the concept of men coming together to achieve a collective task in an organized manner.

When the weak, or powerful yet weak-minded, wield power, there is a high chance that they will practice nepotism in spreading their power to their own kind. Nepotism is the malicious denial of power to those that deserve it in favor of a person who the person in power is close with. A stronghold of inefficiency, weakness, and wrath may be formed. With the weak organized and in positions of power, the truly strong and deserving do not stand a chance in dismantling the system alone in conventional means, because they are not in a position of power to do so. It would take a collective effort outside of the confines of the rules of the system that subjects the powerlessness in order to restore a balance in the power spectrum.

Those with great power may maliciously disseminate power to the squandering weak over the truly deserving in order to maintain their position of power. If power is disseminated to those who will wield it with strength, they might be in a position to overthrow those who are in the position of high power. Power must be disseminated to the strong and deserving for humanity to actualize to its greatest potential. There is no time for waste in incorrect and malicious dissemination and in the wielding of power.

In the destructive imbalance of too much power-seeking or animalistic behavior, only a few have to pursue this excessive nature for the society to be imbalanced and destructive. A society can involve a small part of the population pursuing animalistic behavior and power-seeking behavior while the rest of the population is oblivious and rejects animalistic behavior or power completely. The few and extremely powerful may subject the rest of the population to weakness. A society may be imbalanced with too many people being excessive power-seekers while at the same time being imbalanced with too many people not seeking enough power.

Destructive Societal Imbalance: Not Enough Power Seeking or Animalistic Nature

A societal structure that aims to reject and suppress our animalistic nature or desire to seek power is highly destructive.
A society comprised of people that reject their animalistic nature or reject seeking power is highly destructive.

There is a widespread fallacy in thinking that it is beneficial to our species for our animalistic nature to be completely overcome. This nature is thought of as something that does nothing but hinder and drag down our species into a violent primitive past. Only the fool would ignore our animal nature because it is and should always be ingrained into our being. Our natural desire to reproduce comes from this nature. Using biologically ingrained physical and mental masculine traits, men have built civilizations. Strength has been cultivated over millions of years of evolution to be harnessed and used to build. Our base animal nature is the driving force in the sustenance of our species. Our underlying animalistic nature should not be overcome. It should be controlled and harnessed, not eliminated.

Our animalistic nature is how men remain masculine.
Our animalistic nature is how women remain motherly and feminine.
Our natural desire to reproduce and continue our species is part of our animalistic nature.
Our will to live is part of our animalistic nature.

Retaining an animalistic nature and desiring a certain level of power in oneself are very similar. If the individual rejects the need to obtain power, they deteriorate, just as a depressed person does. Power is needed for the individual to curb depression, to function, to be self-reliant and autonomous, to contribute to and build society, and in the case of men to retain masculinity and remain a sexual being. Power is needed to construct a Self because that is what an individual is- a being that has the power alone to be self-acting.

What does the suppression of animalistic behavior or power do to the individual and society?

The suppression of one's animalistic nature leads to depression. Without an underlying base animal nature, man becomes confused. Maybe the man believes that people are "good" and are now "civilized" and that animalistic traits have no place in humanity and society anymore. Maybe the man is an intellectual and feels that it is silly to retain animalistic traits when his intellectual capacity is beyond animals. Maybe the man is so intellectual that he understands that life is objectively meaningless, so he discards his animalistic side as pointless and useless. After discarding his animalistic nature and embracing meaninglessness, maybe he finds no point in continuing to live. To him blind survival is a simple-minded animal trait. In order to supersede objective meaninglessness, we need a true understanding of the situation, and we also need our animalistic nature. Animals are purely driven to survive, and so should we be driven to survive if we accept that life is worth living. Without this drive to survive and thrive, the man becomes depressed and bogged down by unanswerable questions, or bogged down by the shortcomings of his own self-created weakness. With discarding animalistic nature, the man is also discarding his masculinity, which is a partly innate biological trait. With our biological nature, man has the possibility of cultivating masculinity, but he may deny it. And with denying the necessity to cultivate masculinity the man becomes depressed and weak. Without masculinity and the drive for sex, the man becomes weak and ceases to be a sexual being that pursues real sex and relationships. The lack of sex further exacerbates his depression.

Women who reject their female animalistic side lose their motherliness, and yes, even femininity, which is partly an animalistic trait. The women who I mentioned above who pursue an animalistic nature are not really pursuing a female animalistic nature, but a male one, which completely disregards the creation of a family. If a woman were to follow her female animalistic nature completely, she would desire to select the most dominant male, yet what is conducive to individual and societal success in the animal kingdom is not conducive to success in the kingdom of man. A woman must pursue her female animalistic nature to an extent, retaining motherliness and pursuing a dominant male, but must choose not necessarily a "feasible" man, but a man in which a deep connection may be formed and not a man that is beyond her sexual value, and of course must reject pursuing the animalistic nature of man.

Men who have retained an animalistic nature and masculinity are biologically programmed to desire femininity and submissiveness. If a woman rejects her animalistic side she is rejecting her biologically programmed role in being a feminine and submissive counterbalance to masculine and dominant men. The biological role of women is a very important role in the pairing of mates and counterbalancing of masculinity, as well as for the functioning of the species as a whole. The female animal desires to produce offspring and care for her offspring to the death. Women today who reject their female animalistic side do not desire children, and if they do have children they do not desire to raise and protect them.

The woman who rejects the need to pursue power at all becomes far too submissive, dependent on others, and depressed. Extreme submissiveness, on top of increasing dependence and depression, is also related to hedonism, and the pursuance of hedonism in women is disastrous.

The man who rejects his animalistic side may also see no point in pursuing power after being smacked with the realization that he is an unknowing powerless "nothing" in an absurd existence. Or maybe he believes that power is for "bad" people. He thinks men should act nice to everyone and be nice to women and women will want to be with him because he is a nice guy and everyone will like him because he does not convey any sense of power, which he believes would convey that he is antagonistic and disrespectful. The man may believe that he should not convey whatsoever to a woman that he has an animalistic drive to have sex with her or a drive to be dominant over her. He does this in the hope that the woman will see how nice he is and want to be with him and maybe give him sex eventually if he is not disrespectful. Unfortunately, in denying his animalistic nature and need to cultivate power, that man is never going to have sex, he is never going to be liked by anyone, he is never going to accomplish anything, and he is going to be trampled over. Women want men to be dominant over them. People like people who are confident, know what they need, and don't act superficial. In order to accomplish something a person needs to be able to perform. Other people or externalities will destroy an individual that is not strong enough to fend for themself. Power means that a person has a level of self-respect, self-reliance, autonomy, desires that should be met, and the ability to act and carry out tasks. Society needs men that have cultivated power, not men who rely on everyone else to help them. Without power, one is powerless, and one is weak. Weak people do not contribute as much, and there is no societal-actualization.

Without the understanding of power, one may develop an inferiority complex. People are born with a certain amount of power or status. This is a power placement. Some people are born with better parents, are more intelligent, or have more talent and ability. I believe these things are not necessarily rigid and can be dealt with and changed. But there are some things that an individual cannot change. There is a sexual power placement. Some men are born with better looks, are taller, more masculine, or have a larger penis. All of these things contribute to the sexual value of the man, and they are unchanging or very difficult to change. Masculinity is more of a state of being, yet it is also physical. A man can partially change his physical masculine composition naturally. A man can also partially change his looks. But a man cannot change his height or the size of his dick without surgery. It is important to accept your biology and sexual power placement and your limitations due to it. One must accept the things out of their control but not succumb to their negative consequences and be destroyed by the negative consequences. Through the cultivation of masculinity and reasonable power, a man self-actualizes to his highest potential. This striving for self-actualization is necessary in order to be on the path of building. On the sexual value scale, due to the innate penis size and physical characteristics, a man may have a sexual value of 6 out of 10 and will find it difficult to mate with women 6 and above. Without the cultivation of masculinity and power the man may fall to a sexual value of 3 out of 10. This creates depression and destructiveness. If a man has the potential to have a sexual value of 8 out of 10, but is at 6 out of 10, and the man is with a woman who has had sex with a man that had a value of 7 out of 10, the man can either rise to the challenge and self-actualize, or become defeated with an inferiority complex at his current status and wallow in depression.

When a man thinks it is acceptable to be weak, he ceases to be a man. It is paramount that a man always strives for strength even if he does not attain perfection. It does not matter if one is objectively weak or strong; the striving for strength is the difference between the path of building and destruction. By strength I mean the cultivation of masculinity, confidence, and power.

In our current society many things suppress our animalistic nature and seeking of power. Complete artificiality, oversocialization, political correctness, the acceptance of weakness as virtuous, and the disregard for masculinity are being pushed onto the masses. These things happen to go hand in hand with the liberal ideology and agenda, which I will discuss later.

A society that pursues complete artificiality denies the notion that humanity has any underlying animalistic nature. This misunderstanding has disastrous effects, because we do have an underlying animalistic nature. In the past under complete artificiality women were thought of as non-sexual beings, and it was thought that women desired men who were "nice". It has become well known that women have the capacity to become extremely sexual beings and that women desire men who are dominant, not nice. Not understanding the sexual nature of women leads to a society of men failing to satisfy their women yet existing in a state of clueless satisfaction. Women then become conducive to depression and retaliation. It should be known that not controlling the sexual nature of women also leads to failure and destruction. Artificiality implies ignorance. Understanding is essential. From understanding comes the necessary course.

Oversocialization is excessive artificiality in the social realm. It drives humanity into a box in which people must be overly nice, politically correct, and must use an expansive vocabulary in order to be considered smart and worthy of being heard. It takes power away from people who do not want to be overly nice, do not want to be politically correct, or do not find the need to use large words and ornate communication. Oversocialization is an attempt in totalitarianism of the weak over the strong in order to control the strong. It functions by applying social consequences to those who do not fit the majority of overly socialized people, who may be in positions of power in all areas of society in which their determinations influence other people's careers and lives. Men who are oversocialized are weak, women who are oversocialized are far too dominant.

Political correctness is deadly for a society. Without the power to express oneself in grave and important areas of focus, destruction thrives. Destructiveness has no barriers without the ability for people to communicate dissatisfaction or have the ability to take action on dissatisfaction.

When society pushes men to be weak or makes weakness acceptable, we all suffer, but especially and directly the men. There is no longer any social curbing of male weakness in our society.

A cultivation of a balanced masculinity is a balancing of the power spectrum in men. A man who is masculine, yet not overly masculine, contains all of the traits needed to lead him down the path of building. Courage, resolve, level-headedness, resiliency, confidence, skill, strength. These are all masculine traits. A feminine man does not have any of these traits.

Masculinity in men is one of the most important things to a man and a society, as I will explain further on.

Society has disregarded the need for the retention of masculinity in men. Masculinity is being constricted and men destructively react to this constriction in two ways, wrath or depression. An example of society's constriction on masculinity is the elimination of masculine fields of work or the subjection of men to feminization in work. Men who have to pursue unmasculine fields of work like office work lash out and become power hungry animalistic seekers or accept their fate down the path of feminization. Thus we have the financial industry, full of weak yet power-hungry losers. We see disrespect for men in the trades, which are now regarded as only for stupid low-class men even though those very trades keep society running and keep men masculine. There is no outlet for positive masculine nature in society in general and there is an all-pervasive attack on masculinity. Men are being emasculated.

When men are given the only economical and social option of emasculation, they may reject and leave the "normal" economic and societal structure. Men will leave the normal economic structure if they are not invested in it, if they are destroyed by it, if they feel it makes them weak, if everything is stacked against them, or if their being goes against the grain of society's values (against what society demands). You have gangbangers, homeless men, NEETs (Not educated, employed, or in training) and hermits all rejecting the conventional economy. Gangbangers do not want to be feminized and do not want to prop up a system that seeks to extort them. They then seek power in unconventional ways, and money in unconventional ways. Other factors play into the mindset of the gangbanger but the economy has an influence. Homeless men may exist in madness, but who is to say that it is not they who are mad, but society. NEET's revel in weakness and dependency, yet society offers these men nothing. NEETs are not invested in society and do not agree with society's direction and would rather leach off of it than work hard and suffer for nothing in return. The same goes for hermits, except instead of rejecting the direction of society and the conventional economy and leaching off of it, they desire to separate themselves from society completely and live self-sufficiently alone. All of these men are related by one thing, a lack of positive masculine outlets in work and a dissatisfaction with conventional society- although the dissatisfaction may be for different reasons.

The worst thing that comes with the rejection of

animalistic behavior and power-seeking is sexual degeneration. In a strong society there is a strong polarity between the sexes with men being dominant and masculine, and women being submissive and feminine. But of course with free will, and a society that allows for complete freedom, anything is acceptable. But why should our polar animalistic nature be retained? Proponents of unrestricted free will ask why is it desired for men to remain men and women to remain women when these creations can be dismantled and replaced with something else? Why not continue with our society in which more and more men become feminine and more women become masculine? Why not take it to its conclusion with either a new humanity where all women are the masculine beings and all men are the feminine, or a new humanity comprised of androgynous things?

Our base polar nature should be retained because it is a base guideline to work off of and use as a mental and social anchor, because it is practical, and most importantly because it is necessary.

If the sexes are to be scrambled, this causes immense confusion and suffering. I'm not only talking about suffering with regards to social break down, I am talking about acute mental suffering due to the fact that the person's mind is grating immensely against its true biological nature. Our minds are fragile things and need all of the help they can get from base anchors to work off of in a meaningless existence. The biological polar nature of the sexes is a base mental anchor for individuals to work off of in creating a social structure that forms an individual mental structure.

More importantly, our biological polarity is practical and actualizing. We must harness our biology, not grate against it, distort it, and weaken it. Let men be men and women be women and let them do what they do best. Women are not meant to be men and men are not meant to be women. I do not say this in a religious context, but as a matter of reality and truth. The polar nature of man and woman WORKS. Why destroy something that functions extremely well in creating happiness and productivity? It is hard for men to cultivate masculinity and it is hard for women to cultivate femininity. Yet the rewards are great. People today shrink away from anything that requires effort. Women think men have it much better and want to be men. Men think being a man is too hard and want to be women.

The most important reason for the preservation of masculinity in men and femininity in women is because it is NECESSARY. Social and societal breakdown will occur otherwise. When you tell men it is okay to pursue masculinity and at the same time that it is okay to pursue femininity, you are going to get some very confused people. You are also going to see, over time, the discardation of masculinity in favor of femininity, because it is far easier for a man to relinquish control and power and pursue weakness and submissiveness. On top of the fact that it is completely destructive for a man to pursue weakness, society needs masculine men to keep it functioning. The world is a harsh place and we have not reached our current civilization through weakness. Women contributed to the formation of civilization with their support and counterbalancing of pure masculinity, but it was men who forged civilization out of nothingness with their masculinity. Civilization must be continuously maintained with masculinity. Humanity must use masculinity to survive, civilization or not- especially without a civilization. If for some reason it is collectively decided by all of humanity that the poles should be switched or that there should be no poles, society is done for. The period of transition would be so counterproductive and destructive that humanity would not recover. It takes a strong well-constructed and upheld polar nature of man and woman for society to be on the path of building. As you will see later, the destruction of the polar nature of humanity is the destruction of the family unit, and the family unit is one of the most important elements in the creation of a strong and continuing society and enjoyable life.

Before getting to the creation of a strong family, we first have to look deeper into the nature of sexuality.

Sexuality has to do with power, or the individual's exposure and reaction to external and internal power. The individual can either be sexually dominant or submissive. Humanity's biology is one of sexual dimorphism in which men are the dominant sex and women the submissive, but with free will anything is possible. Environmental factors play a role in a person's sexual development, but in the end it is up to the individual to cultivate the right nature.

Men who are homosexual were likely to be exposed to extremely masculine men (father) counterparted with an extremely submissive mother in which the child would turn to. This manifests later when the child is exposed to masculine boys in which the child feels inferior and turns those feelings into sexual submissive feelings for the boys rather than trying to be masculine himself. The child then turns to approval from his girl peers, just the same as when he turned to his mother who would provide comfort from the domineering overly masculine father. Men who are homosexual may also have had a weak and feminine father in which the child learns and mimics, and never understands the importance of cultivating masculinity. The homosexual man becomes adverse to the harshness of competing for women and the difficulty in cultivating masculinity. The homosexual derives pleasure from being submissive to more dominant men, the path of least resistance in grappling with their inferiority and difficulty.

Men who are "bears" are hyper-masculine and because of this expose themselves to masculinity's fragility and ability to be rejected in favor of deviancy. Hyper-masculinity fosters a snapping of the mind, because it is an extreme state of being that is taxing on the mind and is not objectively necessary. The hyper-masculine man will reach the state of extreme masculinity, realize that even in that state of being there is still always weakness, and turn on this weakness in exploring the subjective free will.

Homosexual men tend to be perfectionists, which explains a lot of their nature. A perfectionist man finds faults in his character easily and exacerbates these faults as objective and absolute truth. For example a homosexual man may have felt that he could not compete with other men for women because of a sense of inferiority. Being a perfectionist, or absolute-minded person, the man's inferiority manifests into a rejection of his masculine nature in which he is not worthy. The man delves into what must be absolutely true- he is inferior to other men and must be submissive to them, and this desire to be submissive grows because it is the path of least resistance. The man rejects the pursuit of women altogether and relishes in his pathetic state of submissiveness by becoming friends with women rather than pursue them sexually- something deep down the man truly desires but suppresses.

Women who are lesbians can be two things:

Dykes are adverse to masculine men because they were exposed to powerful men and developed a feeling of jealously for this power, along with a strong aversion to masculine nature. These women are wrathful. They then try to become men because they feel that they should and CAN be just like men. They want the power of masculinity and they absolutely do not want to be subjected to any masculine power. Masculine women most likely had a weak feminine father or no father, or were brought up to be one of the guys.

The "soft" lesbian is adverse to masculine nature but does not want to become a man, and would rather be submissive to another women then God forbid be submissive to a man and his appendage, the symbol of his masculine nature (His tool of sexual power).

The transgender person is a person that takes the pursuance of their deviant submissiveness or dominance to its logical conclusion. A person may delve into bisexuality, then homosexuality, and there is nothing stopping them from pursuing trans-sexuality. In fact the mind will follow this destructive path because it is the path of least resistance. People support transgender people because they believe that because someone CAN become transgender, they SHOULD become transgender. It is destructive to be transgender and it is destructive to encourage transgender for the sake of the creation and preservation of the self and society, especially regarding the preservation of masculinity. People are not born transgender; they become it. The genetic makeup and/or parental predisposition and early parental influence does have a large effect on the individual's probability of becoming transgender, but the notion that a person is simply born that way is wrong. By genetic makeup I mean that a person is born with certain characteristics that predispose the person to pursuing a deviant path. For example a man can be born with low testosterone and feminine features so he is more likely to pursue homosexuality or become transgender. A woman could be born very large and masculine so would be predisposed to being a dyke or transgender. It is important to always follow the biological nature of masculinity for man and femininity for women no matter what the inclinations of the genetic makeup are.

A reason why a person would pursue sexual deviancy may be because they desire the attention of being different. With the breakdown of social anchors and lack of social curbing, the deviant person recognizes the possibility of being deviant and pursues this deviancy without any repercussion, gaining all of the sympathy of clueless supporters and attention from anyone else.

The acceptance of the cuckold is the end of masculinity and society. When society deems the cuckold acceptable, men turn to its nature because it is the path of least resistance. The cuckold develops and derives a pleasure in being emasculated. The cuckold desires for their woman in their relationship to sleep around with other men of a higher sexual prowess. Proponents of free will argue that it is good for men to pursue cuckoldry because they are getting what they want, pleasure, without harming anyone. A deeper analysis of the situation reveals that the pleasure the cuckold derives is superficial and that a deeper depression is destroying the individual, just the same as any hedonist. The cuckold takes pleasure in their own destruction. The destructiveness of the cuckold situation is so acute because it acutely destroys masculinity and the family unit. Say men of sexual value five relish in their inferiority to men of higher sexual value and pursue cuckoldry. You still have a society with men of sexual value five and higher pursuing masculinity and building society, but what is stopping the wave of cuckoldry to continue until men of sexual value nine desire to be cuckolded by men of even higher sexual prowess. It will continue until the last masculine man on Earth gives up or when civilization collapses, which is something much more likely to occur earlier.

With free will, there is nothing Wrong with being sexually and biologically deviant, but there is something wrong. The allowance of complete free will opens up a society to the destructiveness of the slippery slope and the adverse effects of more and more people becoming abnormal, discarding masculinity, and discarding the path of building.

Controlling our sexuality structures our mind and society and balances our Power and Animalistic Spectrum.

One of the most important components in creating a strong society and enjoyable life is creating strong families. A strong family is the key to creating a strong individual. A balance in the Power and Animalistic/Artificial Spectrums is needed to create a strong family.

When women are "sexually liberated" or "animalistic" they choose to have sex with only the top alpha men as seen above. Add to this the acceptability and even push for hedonism as an intelligent decision and women are even more likely to pursue casual sex with top alpha men. Due to all of this a large percentage of men are not having sex. The men that are having all of the sex are only so many, and they are likely to be animalistic and discard a long-term relationship, so most women do not form families with them. But these women may eventually decide it is in their best interest to settle for a beta provider rather than be alone, so families may still be formed. And so everything works out, everyone is happy, and society is comprised of strong well-formed families. But that is not what actually happens. What happens is the rise of the cuckold culture, in which sexually promiscuous women dominate a relationship with a beta male. The man pursues the nature of the cuckold because there are no other options and it may act as a defense mechanism to an extremely difficult dating situation. Whether or not the relationship becomes a true cuckold relationship in which the women pursues men of higher sexual prowess while using the beta as a provider does not matter. What matters is that the men in these relationships are not dominant and they become weak and submissive. This passes on to the child in which a girl lacks a strong father figure and ends up like the mother, and a boy ends up either weak like the father or despises the father and mother and becomes overly aggressive and animalistic. There are far more and deeper mental problems passed on to the offspring in this family. What needs to happen is women need to control themselves and men need to be strong in order to keep women in check.

A child raised by a single mother has deep mental problems. If the father was not animalistic it is better for a child to be raised by a single father. The reason for the split of the parents may be a combination of the mother being destructive in choosing the wrong mate and the father being destructive in being animalistic. There is a correlation between the father being animalistic and the women becoming a single mother because it is likely she pursued the man for his sexual prowess instead of his ability to be a strong father. Simply put, a boy raised by only a woman never learns from his father how to be a man. The girl raised by only a woman never learns to respect men. The boy never cultivates true masculinity and the girl never cultivates true femininity. The same goes for a child raised by two men or two women. In all of these scenarios the child is brought up in confusion and is exposed to destructive tendencies.

Discarding the current polarity also sends waves of destruction into the social structure of a civilization with regards to the creation of a strong family. If more and more men are going to stop being men, they are going to stop mating with women, completely or in a normal sense. Families will not be formed, or formed in a weak state. Say only 10 men out of 100 remain masculine with the rest being feminine. And say 50 women out of 100 remain feminine with the rest being masculine. Those 10 men will either choose a single mate to form a strong family, or choose multiple women in which the family would be weaker. The 50 masculine women are most likely lesbians, but regardless the 10 masculine men would not want to have anything to do with them. Those women must choose from the 90 feminine men or do not form families. The 90 feminine men are not selected by any of the feminine women. They either do not form a family or mate with a dominant woman. There is the possibility of only 10 strong families being formed, in which the polar nature is passed on. Masculinity is not preserved.

What does a balancing of the two spectrums accomplish in creating a strong society?

Pillars of a Strong Society:
-Encouraging self-control, courage, wonder, humor as opposed to the 5 destructors, but more specifically...

1. Social guidelines, creating:
     -Various social and mental anchors in order to carry out day-to-day life and interactions.
          Society is built on the curbing of our natural destructive and animalistic desires. It is built on cooperation and control.
     -Interactions that strengthen bonds between people not destroy them.
          Enjoyment of life by connecting and forming relationships with people.
     -Masculinity in men
     -Femininity in women
     -The Family Unit

2. A driving motive to build and strengthen a civilization out of chaos and nothingness:
     -Productivity
          Contentment with one's existence and society makes for a productive person.
     -Individual Autonomy
          Having power and freedom.
     -Cooperation between individuals
          Social cohesion is needed for actualization.

Section 4: A World Completely Off the Mark

Society, the great pillar that humanity needs to be true and strong in order to be on the path of building, is currently ruinous, and a ruinous society puts humanity on the path of destruction. The collective conscious of humanity is wrong and this manifests into a society that is totally awry. Humanity must unite as one collective force in order to actualize our potential. We cannot be fragmented because a fragmented foundation will collapse.

There exist people in our society who seek to understand the world and fight for humanity to become actualized to its potential, whether they are conscious of their nature or not. A person does not need to be consciously aware of specific things like "the duality of human nature" or anything that I have said in this essay in order to be a builder. Yet all of the efforts that builders make in strengthening society mean nothing if the destructiveness of the masses washes away their contributions and drags humanity into the pit and path of destruction. The root of all destructiveness is ignorance and this is what our ruinous society is built on.

Overwhelming destructiveness negates building, and an overwhelmingly destructive society seeps into those that build. People who desire to build society up may consciously or subconsciously be aware of the decadence of its current state and may lose hope. Even though it is the individual who chooses to be destructive, society may push and drive the individual into destructiveness.

The destructiveness of society may be so strong and entrenched that some people may venture deeper into destructiveness and desire to push for the destruction of society in order to end their suffering and take society out with them in a complete loss of hope for all of humanity.

Some people may believe that contributing to the complete destruction of society may end its reign quicker and a new society can be built on top of its ashes. The wild destruction of areas of society or all of society may seem to be the right thing to do, but this only sets humanity back. You can rebuild a society at any time; it does not take total collapse to do so. Total collapse brings unnecessary suffering and waste. With total collapse you only drag humanity into total despair, and this is difficult to recover from. Driving humanity into the deepest depths of destructiveness only makes it harder to rebuild. You can reconstruct a society at any time and you can salvage all that is strong and beneficial while discarding all destructiveness. Deconstruction and reconstruction in certain areas is far greater than the complete annihilation and rebuilding of society from scratch. Builders must be firm in their ways and united in a collective force. Nothing will get accomplished, both in complete destruction or complete building, if builders are fighting at the same time for the annihilation and salvaging of society. Those that desire annihilation and then rebuilding are no longer on the path of building.

If society is to be strong, I call for every human being to rise from the slumber of complacency and ignorance and elevate humanity to its potential until the end of human existence. If life is worth it for us, it shall be worth it for our descendants. If the choice is made for humanity to continue, we shall exist for all of eternity. The collective conscious will remain in existence and with it all of the lives of every human being that has ever existed intertwined with the future and destiny of our species.

People must take action. People must organize. Indifference shall no longer exist. The builders of our time shall no longer be silenced and neglected. I have created this foundation for others to take the torch of truth into the future. I call for truth-seekers to rise and carry this torch.

I call for the controlled deconstruction of many aspects of society, and a reconstruction of these areas in the way of building.

Society must be made strong and true in these areas for the actualization of our species.

The Concept of Sustainability

If the point of this essay is to get across that it is not worth it for humanity to go out in a fast loud destructive bang, then long-term thinking and sustainability must be primary focuses and objectives. Building is not done overnight, it is done steadily over a long period of time, and it never ends. As long as there is life, there must be building and maintaining. This means that nothing should be done hastily for quick benefits with short or long-term destruction. Things should not be neglected, things should not be taken advantage of, things must be well thought out, things must be managed with understanding and discipline.

The individual must be sustainable and society must be sustainable in all areas. This means that economics and business practices must be sustainable.

Individualism/Collectivism

A lot of what I have talked about revolves around how the individual should deal with the "other" or "external". My philosophy can be described as a balancing of individualism and collectivism. Individualism recognizes that the individual is the sole actor in their subjective plane of existence and is responsible for their actions, that a strong formation of self is needed, and that individual autonomy and needs must be met. Collectivism recognizes that individuals do not exist in a vacuum and must interact with others for the benefit of the individual and all. Social cooperation and cohesion are important and individual sacrifice must be made for the greater collective good.

The importance is in balancing these two natures.

Government

Government provides structure for a society. Individuals need a government to provide an enforced set of values and rules to live by, and to provide leadership for collective tasks as well as providing organization in order to complete the tasks that would be too difficult to organize without the governmental structure.

A government can be formed in many ways and government officials can come into power many ways.

In America, like most of the world, most government officials are elected by democratic election. Democracy is not the greatest form of government, but it shall do for now. A society led by the greatest truth-seeking builders (philosopher kings as Plato would say) is the best form of government. Not only would they be the most efficient rulers by their merit, if simply chosen and brought into power by a handful of qualified people this would be a government unmatched in efficiency. No time would be wasted in campaigning, voting, or squabbling between people vying for positions of power; the right man would seek the position and would be chosen after deliberation by a few people. There would be no conflict, the best man would be chosen for the job and the other men who tried to go for the position would understand and step down. All positions in government would be selected by merit, not through political maneuvers or nepotism. The greatest truth-seeking builders at the helm of government would have absolute power. This absolute power is the freedom to make decisions in all areas necessary to do so. This form of government can only be put into action if the duality of human nature is understood by all.

In a democracy or any government, a society needs strong individuals who are without any destructive tendencies to run the government. A government and society also needs citizens who do not take advantage of the government with their destructive tendencies like weakness, excessive power-seeking, or indifference.

The most important thing in running a government is that people have to be involved and care about how their government is run, and care about strengthening society. If the government body is elected by democracy, it is important for people to be involved in the government, and not let it deteriorate through negligence. Politicians cannot be motivated by self-interest or the interest of the few or corrupt, they must strive for the strengthening of society. Strong philosophical leaders must vie for political positions. If a person is dissatisfied with the crop of politicians, and believes they are capable of being a strong philosophical leader, it is their duty to vie for political positions and not expect the weak and corrupt to be capable of anything beneficial. The people who do not vie for positions must be involved in their society and their government by speaking with elected officials, proposing ideas, speaking with others about what the government is doing, and voting. Apathy is the death of a government and society.

Efficiency is paramount in an effective government, as inefficiency can quickly take hold in government and deteriorate a society. Inefficiency arises easily in a government because there is a lack of oversight, accountability, or direct consequence. A government should be efficient in completing tasks or providing services, and should limit the amount of time and resources needed to complete these tasks.

Bureaucracies strive for efficiency and order, but instead increase complexity, create inefficiency, and dehumanize everyone involved. Bureaucracies should be done away with and humanity should be brought back into government. Government workers need the power and freedom to perform tasks and get things done without the necessity of complete rigidness. One of the problems of bureaucracies is that they facilitate the expansion of government and an expansion of government facilitates bureaucracies.

The government must serve its base goal and not

grow out of control and extend into every aspect of people's lives. The encroachment of the government into meddling, controlling, and monitoring every aspect of people's lives attempts to curb people's free will into non-destructiveness and order, but with excessiveness it negates free will completely and creates far more destructiveness. As beings with total free will, we need freedom, or the allowance to act in free will without repercussion in non-destructive areas. Without freedom the individual will feel constrained and will explode in retaliation with excessive and destructive free will. The individual needs autonomy and the enjoyment of freedom.

Some government control is necessary in curbing people's actions and stopping people who exhibit extremely destructive behavior for the preservation of society, but to think that government, and an expanding government, is the solution to people exhibiting destructiveness is narrow-minded and fatal. We have created a society that constrains and restricts and denies people's need for freedom outside of the government. The solution to people's dissatisfaction and display of extreme freedom is not to increase the size of the government, it is to increase the size of freedom in society outside of the government and decrease within the government when the restriction is too overbearing.

As societies clash on the global scale, we need global understanding of the duality of human nature, not a race to see who can expand their military. A nation must be able to defend itself against threats, but balance is needed. Understanding is the only way to solve societal clash in the long run, and it cannot be simply the understanding of one side's ideas or the other, it must be a mutual understanding of the duality of human nature.

The encroachment of the government in taking all of the citizens' money for use of government activities that are not essential or are actively destructive extinguishes the individual will to contribute to the government or society. Why would an individual want to contribute to a government that is destroying society in waste and ignorance? All non-essential government activities should cease, as the government is no place to conduct them.

In America there must be a decrease in power and spending in the federal government. There must be a wide elimination of government programs along with the complete elimination of government grants, which are completely useless and actively destructive. A government should serve the bare minimum of what is required of it in terms of creating a functioning society, not waste money provided by hard-working people in frivolous, useless, and actively destructive avenues of waste, idiocy, and malice. There must be a complete dismantling of the government's current power and scope, and the government must be made small, simple, and in control of the American people. Government employees should be paid far less with far less benefits. As people toil in uncertain employment with low pay, government workers are paid exorbitant salaries directly from these workers to frolic in cushy offices doing barely any work at all. Lobbying props up destructive corporations and organizations while feeding greedy power hungry corrupt disloyal pathetic politicians. Corporate lobbying must end and lobbying as we know it today must be completely dismantled. The American government is an entangled mess of corruption, self-interest, overcomplexity, waste, and is a complete disgrace. Washington DC must be overhauled.

Politics

Politics is rooted in philosophy. Here I analyze the two major political parties of America.

-Conservatives have an unbalanced power spectrum with too much allowance for power-seeking.
-Conservative side is unconscious of animalistic nature which is dangerous, but involves limiting our sexual animalistic nature. Became too limiting at times in the past in which

artificiality became a problem.
-Many so-called conservatives are actually sexually degenerate animalistic individuals.
-Conservatives have an imbalanced animalistic survival of the fittest mentality.
-Conservatives lack an understanding of the need for collective cooperation.

-Conservatives understand the need for cultivating power.

-Liberals do not understand power at all, resulting in weakened individuals and the creation of all sorts of fucked up cocked-eyed shit involving people who do not deserve power being granted too much power, and people who need and deserve power not being granted that power.
-Liberal side involves the allowance for too much individual and social freedom resulting in animalistic behavior and destruction from primarily ignorance, hedonism, and degeneracy. Liberal ideas produce depression in men and women and wrath in men and women for separate but related reasons. Allows for too much social freedom without recognizing the consequences because there is not an understanding of our underlying nature or the necessities in creating a functioning society.
-Liberals dismiss masculinity.
-Liberals favor the expansion of government.
-Liberals are excessive power seekers determined in dominating anyone that stands in the way of their destructive totalitarian agenda.

-Liberals understand the need for collective cooperation.

Building can be found within a combination of the strengths in thinking of both parties.

Economics

An economic system that aligns with and harnesses the core nature of human existence and rejects destructiveness is needed for humanity to be on the path of building.

This system would recognize the need for each individual to obtain power and would harness the individual will to obtain power, but it would involve rejecting excessiveness in extortion and hoarding. To combat excessive power seeking through hoarding, people in power must allow for the offloading of power in money and ownership to others that deserve it, along with consumers rejecting businesses run by excessive power-seekers. Power cannot be offloaded to those who do not deserve the power though. These are people who will relinquish all responsibility from themselves and will not work hard or work at all.

All of this achieves a balance in the power spectrum, the key to building.

The economic system I have created that strives for complete building is called Conscious Capitalism. It is beyond capitalism, and it is beyond any economic system ever devised in the history of mankind. It is beyond any system because it supersedes rigid structure and is based in personal choice, cooperation and nuance. This economic system is individualism and collectivism intertwined in their strongest forms.

Individuals must extract resources, create goods, and provide services for the continuation of the species. Individuals may either own the means of production and be compensated by consumers with money for what they provide, or individuals work for someone who owns the means of production as a means of production in exchange for money. The means of production are resources, equipment, and labor. The person who works for themself and provides only their labor has ownership of the means of production. If the person works for someone else it can be said that the employer owns the person's labor as a means of production and can direct the person as they please until the point where the worker chooses to leave.

Ownership of resources and equipment is one thing; the individual must have the drive to turn those resources (knowledge may be a resource) and equipment into a good or service. Most of the drive comes from the compensation in money they will receive from consumers. An employee must also have the drive to work for someone else. Most of the drive to work for someone else comes from the compensation they receive from the employer. These drives are essential to action and creation. If a person does not have the drive or funds to start their own business, they must offer themselves as a means of production for someone else. As a means of production they simply have to complete their specific tasks and do not have to worry about running the entire organization or providing funds for it, but they do not get a share of the profits, they do not have any power, and the locus of power over their responsibilities and pay is with the owner. The owner is free to take advantage of the worker up to the point that the worker leaves the organization.

When business owners hoard their power, the rest of the population is forced into a position of powerlessness in which they must offer themselves as only means of production because they do not have the access to resources or equipment, do not have the funds to acquire them, and it is difficult for them to create a business with little money because the established businesses use their power to increase productivity and out compete any newcomers. Those who are not the owners are driven into servitude and taken advantage of because the owner CAN take advantage of them, and because it is thought that they MUST in order to maximize profit. The imbalance created in hoarding is complete destructiveness. A life of servitude is a life that is not worth living. A person who feels that their life would be worth living if the system were different develops destructive tendencies because the system is so large and complex that a controlled deconstruction of the system is impossible for a lone person.

78

Business owners must also be consumers, but since there is a small percentage of business owners and an extremely large percentage of people who are not, it can be said that the workers are also the consumers. Business owners may take advantage of the consumer, even more so when there is less competition in the field or if there is collusion in the field. Prices may be exorbitantly raised and profits do not go to the worker (consumer), it goes directly to the owners.

Business owners, the controllers of operation, may abuse workers and they may also abuse the resources and the consumer. The owner may abuse the environment, abuse animals, and use practices that create a poor product, or even a harmful product. The consumer may be unaware of the treatment of workers, unaware of the abuse of resources, and unaware of the abuse they receive if the product they are given is deceptively poor or harmful. Businesses may be able to hide the destructiveness of the operation or product through advertising or by keeping their mouth shut. In most cases there are no repercussions for businesses that operate destructively.

The best economy is one in which every individual is driven to contribute and build, and everyone enjoys their life. It is an economy that minimizes destructiveness and maximizes building.

The individual may be in one of four roles in the economy, and in each of these roles they have the free will and choice to act either destructively or constructively. The owner, worker, consumer and government must work together in order to build.

The Business Owner-

It is up to the individual to create a business that is not destructive. The individual mind must understand that money maximization is not the goal. Building is the goal, and society as a whole must be included in this goal.

In order to minimize destructiveness and maximize building, the business owner must take a small profit instead of seeking the maximization of profit for themself. The business owner should pay their workers their worth and should provide their services to consumers for a reasonable price, while keeping a small profit in compensation. With pure capitalism the owners of businesses instead desire to push wages down to the bare minimum amount required to keep an active labor force and price their services to consumers in a way to acquire the most profit possible. Pure capitalism rewards greed and excessive power-seeking. But as one individual obtains power at another's expense, the other person develops wrath or depression. An excessive power-seeker does not use their power to create more power in others, they hoard their power and wield it to obtain even more power. Yet if a business owner is not compensated for their risks in obtaining power and producing goods, they will become wrathful or depressed. A balance is needed.

Individuals must desire and obtain power, but not too much power, and individuals who obtain power must disseminate the power to others. The dissemination of power must be done in an efficient manner that maintains productivity and does not interfere with the others' will to obtain power. Weakness is created if power is disseminated to those who do not deserve it or will squander it. The inefficient dissemination of power usually does not come from the business owners, but from the government seizing the power and distributing it to the masses. In order to disseminate power efficiently it must come from the owner directly to the worker, in the form of money, ownership and respect.

If Conscious Capitalism is to work, the basis of the economy is the formation of respectful relationships. Without strong relationships, individuals are turned into interchangeable cogs and treated poorly. Without a respectful relationship with the world, people will neglect it and destroy it. The formation of relationships starts with the business owner. Workers must be treated with respect and not subjected to poor working conditions, or if they are, compensated fairly for them. A worker must be paid fairly, with sacrifice being made by the owner, and as you will see later, the consumer. Owners should strive to create a more enjoyable and fulfilling work experience. Workers should not be treated as cogs, performing simplified, degrading and monotonous tasks over and over. The worker should be involved in the creation of a product or service in an extensive role, and see the fruits of their labor. A more extensive role means more power is being granted to the person, so that person must step up to the challenge.

The allocation of ownership is essential. Ownership means power and a share of the profits. Without the dissemination of ownership the imbalance of power becomes out of control. With regards to passing on a business, family is important, but always allocating ownership from one familial generation to the other is too simplistic. If a business remains a small entity that can be managed by a small family it makes sense to pass it on within the family. But if a business can support multiple families, then it is destructive to keep that business controlled by one family, reaping all of the profits.

It is up to the business owner to not take advantage of consumers or the planet. Consumers may be swayed into buying destructive products. Advertisements influence these people into buying into their own ignorance. Destructive industries must be done away with.

It is up to the business owner to keep their business on a small scale and not hoard all the power of the market or industry for themselves. A sacrifice must be made to allow other businesses to form. The focus should be on keeping a business local and if there is room for expansion an allocation of ownership to another person is necessary.

Businesses must not operate for the sole sake of making money. This mentality creates a lot of the destructiveness within an economy. Businesses must be made in order to strengthen society and every individual within.

When a business ceases to operate for the sole sake of making money, it may become less profitable and risk being out competed by businesses that do seek to maximize profit and cut cost, but we will see later how this is remedied with the choice of the consumer.

The Worker-

The worker must seek power and responsibility, and when allocated power the worker must wield that power with strength.

In Conscious Capitalism the individual is responsible for obtaining their livelihood. A little help is provided by the government, which I will go into later. If an individual does not cultivate worth then they do not deserve power and money. Workers must seek to become entrepreneurial and must seek responsibility rather than shy away from it. If an individual does not want responsibility then they do not deserve any share of ownership and a cut of the profits.

The individual must know his place in society and in the economy. People must be graceful and know their limitations, power placement, and limit their greed for power. People must know that contributing to the building and maintenance of society can be done in ways that are not as direct and are less fulfilling, but are still beneficial and necessary. People must find their piece in the puzzle of society and must seek occupations that contribute to building and truth seeking, no matter how far removed from it. Caring for others is a piece of the puzzle. Maintenance is a piece of the puzzle. People must know their place.

The worker goes down the path of destruction if they become too greedy, jealous, or lazy.

The Consumer-

The consumer plays a major role in making Conscious Capitalism function. In the end, it is up to the conscious individual to choose to support either destructive businesses or businesses that strengthen society for all. A sacrifice must be made by the consumer in the form of paying a higher price in order to support businesses that do not operate destructively. In the end the payoff for supporting certain businesses (this is where nuance comes in) is far greater than the money saved in supporting a destructive business and economic system.

A business that operates destructively exploits the worker, consumer, and Earth. The consumer may still feel it is necessary to play into the game of the exploitation of themselves because they believe there are no other options. The consumer may also be oblivious to there own exploitation. The consumer that does not care about the worker does not have any empathy, common sense, or understanding of what it takes to build society. The consumer who facilitates the exploitation of the worker is no better than the business owner that exploits. Consumers do not comprehend that they are also workers. It is in their best interest to support the actualization of other workers for the sake of the widespread benefits that come around to themselves.

According to the doctrine of modern economics, with economies of scale, large corporations are able to cut costs and sell their products to consumers cheaper. Under the same doctrine, the consumer should buy the cheapest product and support the most efficient business to save money and in turn support a system that uses resources efficiently. Except common economics and economical thinking does not consider the larger picture. Unconscious consumers choose to support businesses in the component that is most visible, their ability to produce a product efficiently and cheaply. Yet this ability does not make the certain business the best choice. If a consumer supports the corporate economic structure, they are supporting their own indirect demise. They may get their goods cheaper, but they must also work for cheaper for the same corporations that control the economy. Large corporations are soulless- they have no concept of rejecting destructiveness and choosing building. Individuals become faceless cogs in the corporate machine and are treated that way.

A strong overall economy is one in which the focus is on strengthening the smaller-scale economies of the communities within it by supporting small local businesses. This economy is also one in which money is not allocated to entities that extort and exploit. With a small-scale economy you have the opportunity to form relationships, keep a closer check on how the business operates, and trust in a local business run by people you can interact with. By supporting a small local business you are more likely to get a well-crafted or tailored high quality product and you support the self-actualization of the workers and business owners who choose to operate in the way of building. By supporting the community economy a person supports the community's ability to be self-reliant, along with helping each individual in that community to become self-reliant. Self-reliance is incredibly important in the formation of a strong individual and for its practicality in strengthening communities against the turbulence of the larger world.

Small businesses have a greater opportunity to allocate power to its workers more easily.
Small businesses have a better opportunity to not extort the workers or consumers.
Small businesses are less likely, by their nature or by their operation, to have less of an impact on the environment and on the aesthetic of the environment.

With a small-scale local economy you keep the money local and in the hands of people you can trust and who do not exploit. By supporting large-scale corporations you give money to an entity that extracts money from one area and allocates excessive profits to people living elsewhere. There is less oversight in dealing with large corporations and less of an ability to influence their destructiveness. The consumer must invest in small locally owned businesses. It is counterproductive to join into the corporate economic scheme by putting money into the status quo corporate stock market. The corporate status quo is status quo because it is pushed onto the masses and because it is the easiest and less risky way to make money. The individual must look at the origin of fast-money making and must look beyond quick profits. Special care must be made in choosing the right small local business to invest in because these businesses are less of a guaranteed money generator.

In a system of capitalism, there cannot be an excessive artificial propping up of non-destructive businesses that do not operate effectively. There must be competition or else the use of resources is inefficient. The individual will to compete and produce the greatest most efficient product must be preserved. It is also to the benefit of society that some industries simply will have to remain large-scale as well. In these industries there is less room for the self-actualization of workers and large-scale efficiency is highly practical. These businesses should be the last to be converted into smaller-scale counterparts, but there should still be focus in eliminating all destructiveness in operation and if necessary, scale. The conversion of industries to small-scale will not happen overnight.

The Government-

Individuals comprise and shape the government, which acts on the economy. The government is used to counteract the destructiveness of the economy. The use of the government to curb destructiveness is inefficient and even counterproductive.

The government is inefficient in curbing human nature because it is up to the individual to choose for themself if they want to act destructively or not. Forcing someone to act a certain way grates against the individual and makes the individual desire to exercise their free will in defiance.

Inequality and an imbalance of power is part of human nature and society. Pure socialism or communism rejects this nature and creates weakness and dependency. The concept of absolute allocation for equality may create weakness in the individual or society.

The government should function as a limited cushion for individuals that need short-term help. Individuals that need help with providing for their sustenance should be provided with a very limited base sustenance, not salary, in order to keep a smoothly operating society while protecting against creating weak and dependent individuals. The government should partially tackle income inequality by instituting a modest scaled taxation with special emphasis on taxing the very rich.

Government regulation of business operation should be minimized in areas that only function as red tape. In areas of regulation that truly reduce destructiveness the government should exercise nuance in keeping regulation against extreme destructiveness while instituting a slow minimization of regulation in other areas to make way for freedom as individuals awaken to the duality of human nature.

As part of eliminating economic power inequalities, government employees, white collar or otherwise, should be paid one half, one third, or less of their current salaries and benefits depending on how exorbitant their salaries are. The government should not act as a corporation that extorts the population and allocates exorbitant salaries to workers of the government.

A combination of efforts from consumers, workers,

owners, and government is needed to eliminate usury and the corporate financial industry. A collective effort is also needed to balance the power spectrum in white-collar and blue-collar positions, in which power is heavily allocated to the white-collar side. A collective effort is needed in supporting masculine areas of work and in preserving masculinity in jobs rather than eliminating them with technology. Finally a collective effort is needed to reject the notion that the economy can function as a continual growth model.

Usury is evil (wrathful and destructive) and must be eliminated. Very low interest rates are okay, but no interest is even better.

People must not put their money into the corporate financial system and members of the corporate financial system must cease to operate. The corporate financial industry takes huge profits and allocates money to large corporations. The financial industry produces nothing of value, is full of greed and useless wastefulness, and actively destroys society. This is reflected in the personalities of those that comprise the industry- empty and soulless. People must stop giving money and power to Wall Street and the globalist corporate elite.

Real work must be compensated, not paper-pushing uselessness. A hard physical labor position can be considered more fulfilling than the office life but it is incorrect to say that because of this, office jockeys should be compensated more. A hard physical labor position is objectively more difficult than a white-collar office job. A masculine man would need to be paid far more to get him to do an office job, but for the large percentage of people an office job is much more appealing than doing strenuous physical labor. Should an office full of women be paid more than a work yard full of men? Many office jobs are actually not that soul-crushing and are fulfilling anyways. Work should be compensated for its real value and for what it takes for people to want to do the job. Useless paper pushers should not be compensated far more than a blue-collar worker simply because it is less desirable of a job. Less desirable does not mean compensated more than every other job, although it does play a factor.

An effort must be made to supersede the inevitability of technology supplanting all work, and especially masculine areas of work. This must be done through all four roles in the economy. There needs to be a growing respect and support of the masculine worker and builder.

I will end the section on economics by saying that the idea of constant growth is impossible and destructive because we live on a planet of limited resources and many people. The common economic doctrine of continual economic growth must be discarded for an economy that is sustainable and on the path of building.

Agriculture

Agriculture provides people with a more efficient and reliable supply of food through the organization and centralization of crops and animals. With the centralization of food, our species discarded the nomadic lifestyle and instead people chose to settle in one location. The small community was formed and the rest is history. If agriculture created the community thousands of years ago, a certain type of agriculture today has helped destroy it.

There are two types of agriculture:

Conventional and/or industrial farming is destructive. Small-scale family-owned local organic farming is constructive.

Conventional farming is the growing of crops with the use of pesticides and other chemicals, the raising of animals with hormones and additives, and it encompasses industrial agriculture, which is the cultivation of large amounts of land with large machinery and advanced technology. Conventional farms do not have to be industrial, but industrial farming is conventional. The use of chemicals and technology allows the conventional farm to cut costs and price their product cheaper, attracting consumers and expanding their market share, with the possibility of transporting and selling their product far distances. Small conventional farms may be owned and operated by a family with hired workers, but most medium to large conventional farms are owned by large corporations and operated by people hired by the corporation. Conventional farming seems harmless doesn't it?

Small-scale family-owned local organic farming, or "small-scale" farming, is firstly the cultivation of crops or animals on a small parcel of land with organic practices. Small-scale means that large machinery or advanced technology is not used. Organic cultivation or raising does not involve pesticides or hormones. These practices are used to preserve a more natural environment, the long-term productivity of the soil, and the health of the animals and consumers. These farms are owned and operated by a family with minimal help from hired workers. These farms mostly sell directly to community members nearby. A farm that uses organic practices, but is on a large-scale with large machinery and corporate ownership is industrial and conventional, even though they do not use pesticides.

Conventional farming has become the dominant form of farming in the world and in America. Capitalism has enabled industrial and conventional farming to take hold because it favors productivity and power hoarding. The economic system is the facilitator of the rise of industrial farming, but one of the roots is the widespread and all pervasive idea that it is beneficial and Right for industrial farming to replace small-scale farming. It is thought that alleviating farmers from working physically is a great step in alleviating suffering while bringing cheap food to the masses. It is thought that technological progress and efficiency are God, and farmers that desire to work on a small-scale and use inefficient practices are outdated or even evil. There is an all-pervasive disrespect of hard-working farmers, and masculine lines of work in general, possibly because people are insecure in their state of dependence, weakness, and femininity. Small-scale farmers and the farming lifestyle are being discarded by society. The favoring of conventional farming comes at a great cost, a cost that is not factored into the cheapness of the products that conventional farming produces. The greatest destructor of small-scale farming is pure narrow-mindedness and obliviousness. I hope to eradicate this narrow-mindedness and obliviousness in these next few paragraphs. With regards to the small-scale farmers themselves, I urge them to listen to Wendell Berry who has influenced my perception on agriculture and the world greatly. He said, "It may be that the gravest danger to farmers is their inclination to look to the government for help, after the agribusiness corporations and the universities (to which they have already looked) have failed them. In the process, they have forgotten how to look to themselves, to their farms, to their families, to their neighbors, and to their tradition."

Conventional farming is destructive for environmental reasons. Pesticides eliminate all insect and animal life in an area and force these critters into other areas, even onto nearby organic farms. Poor practices with large machinery and skipping the use of crop covering during the winter creates the runoff of soil at large rates across the planet. Good soil is not something that is just regenerated on a piece of land, once it leaves and enters the rivers and ocean the only way to regain good soil is to bring it from somewhere else, a costly feat. Large industrial farms destroy the landscape and replace lush thriving ecosystems with desolate fields that stretch for miles and miles. This is something that has obvious effects on wildlife and the physical landscape, but it should also be known that it also has an effect in the mindset of the individual, which I will discuss in the section on environment.

One of the most important but overlooked components of conventional farming is the long-term destruction and reduction in productivity of the topsoil. Pesticides eliminate the microbial life and insect life of the soil. Without microbial and insect life the soil becomes barren and is not conducive to producing. Pesticides and genetic engineering also create superbugs and superweeds that become more and more resistant to the herbicides and pesticides. With this more toxic pesticides and herbicides must be used creating environmental and especially productivity problems. With the use of conventional monoculture, disease becomes more prevalent, the soil erodes quicker, and the productivity of the soil diminishes. Large machinery destroys and compacts soil.

There are health problems associated with the use of pesticides. Pesticides are toxic and when they come into contact with farm workers it affects their health. Studies have shown that exposure to pesticides causes rashes, blisters, stinging eyes, blindness, nausea, dizziness, headaches, coma, and death in the short-term. Long-term effects include infertility, birth defects, endocrine disruption, neurological disorders, and cancer. The consumer ingests the poisonous substances if care is not taken in washing the produce well. The pesticides may never be able to be removed from the produce nor are they removed from the air. Pesticides may contaminate all of the nearby area of a conventional farm. Exposure to pesticides creates serious health issues both in the short and long term, especially to conventional farmworkers who are clearly disregarded and treated as subhuman.

Small-scale farming creates and preserves lush environments and soil that are full of life. Crop covering and crop rotation are used. Small fields are cultivated with small tractors or with the use of horses. No pesticides are used and instead organic matter is introduced into the soil to create incredibly productive soil. With a small-scale operation insects and animals can be managed with more ease and care. A small-scale farm is very likely to be a diversified operation with both plants and animals, creating a sustainable and self-reliant operation. The animals provide manure that can be added to the soil and the plants can feed the animals.

Conventional farming puts too much power into the hands of the few. Our conventional agriculture system is run by giant corporations that hire farm managers and workers to operate the farm. These managers and workers are paid well below their worth and they are treated poorly. They are worked to death for little compensation and all of the enormous profits go to the owners and white-collar workers of the corporation.

The quality of life for those that work on an industrial mechanized farm is little. The farmer and worker on this farm are cogs in a machine, not part of a natural, balanced, and enjoyable way of life on a small-scale farm. There is no enjoyment of work and no satisfaction in labor. Farmworkers and farmers have the highest rate of suicide of any occupation in America. At one time farmers believed that it was worth it to farm, work hard, and support the entire population in sustenance. These farmers cared about society and life. But with conventional farming, the operators of a farm do not care about life and they do not care about a society that disrespects and discards them. If society wants food and wants farmers, then the farmers must be in control of their lives. There is no other way; a farmer cannot be removed from the ownership and direct care of the land. This removal is responsible for the widespread disregard for the land, because there is no tight relationship between these operators that work for someone else on someone else's land, and who receive orders from these removed owners, who are not involved with any actual farming. The industrial farm is a complete abomination.

What we have is a widespread destruction of the family farm. People have considered only one thing in farming, economics, and society; profits. Efficiency and technology have taken over and human beings have been taken out of the farmland. It is thought that it is good and smart to remove people from farms because their work is difficult. This is extremely clueless and wrong. The family farm is a way of life and it is a great way of life. Society has first destroyed the family and with it the family farm. A society must save the family in order to save the family farm. The family farm is self-reliant and self-actualizing. There is a deep contentment in life for a family that works hard and sees the fruit of their labor, all the while remaining in control over their lives. The power-hungry elites in our society may be working against the family farm because it represents freedom and power. With the destruction of the family farm in favor of technology we also see the destruction of masculinity. Is efficiency really worth the destruction of one of the cornerstones of an enjoyable life for a man? What I see, in one simple idea in switching back to the small-scale family farm, is the creation of a self-actualizing society composed of happy, strong, self-reliant families, the preservation of masculinity, the necessary allocation of power, the preservation of the soil and land, and finally the recreation of the community.

The community has not been solely destroyed by a change in agriculture to conventional, but a change back in agriculture to small-scale farming may greatly help restore it. Large conventional farms are wastelands. They are incredibly large and spread out. They feed giant supermarkets in which people go, get their food, and go home. There is no community of nearby farmers interacting with each other and interacting with consumers, or consumers interacting with each other. Everyone is alone. With the restoration of the small-scale farm we have thriving agricultural communities with connected sociable farmers interacting with each other and the consumer, and we have the farmer's market, a great venue for obtaining local food and being sociable with everyone in the community. The farmer's market is an event and there is room for far more events when people come together in connection with food.

With small-scale farming the community becomes

self-sufficient and does not need the support of outside sources. There is great power and value in being self-sufficient. The turbulence and control of outside sources on an entity, the community in this case, weighs on the powerless entity. Self-sufficient communities also eliminate great waste in transporting goods across far distances. There is a large reduction in oil consumption. Small-scale family owned local organic farms should be the foundation for a community's food supply. The creation of strong independent communities is vital for the success of society at large.

It is up to the consumers to choose the path of building and choose the small-scale farm, but there is one other great obstacle in the success of the small-scale farm. The government is destroying the small-scale farm and propping up the industrial farm corporations. The Iron Triangle of farm corporation lobbyists, Congress, and the Department of Agriculture work together, in each of their own self-interest, to support the large industrial farming industry. Lobbyists buy influence and elections, the House and Senate committee and sub-committees of agriculture provide favorable legislation for the lobbyists and funding for governmental agriculture agencies, and the Department of Agriculture provides money and support for the farm corporations and legislators. The so-called "experts" in agriculture in government and universities are malicious and useless. The Iron Triangle must be ended and enormous sums of subsidies and support towards the industrial farm must end.

Environment

We are a part of nature, not separate from it.
We are a part of the environment, not separate from it.
We must harness and take care of the environment, not abuse and destroy it (ourselves)- just as we must harness and be in control of our biological human nature.
Humanity shapes the environment and the environment shapes humanity both in physical aesthetic and in what the

environment provides.
Humanity must make an effort to use the environment and create the environment with intelligence.
Humanity must make an effort to preserve the untouched environment in some places.
The destruction of the natural environment is destructive towards humanity.
The creation of an unpleasant physical aesthetic is detrimental to humanity.

Humanity is a part of nature, not separate from it. If we are nature, then we must work with nature and not battle it or abuse it. We must not be overcome by the negative consequences of nature, which means we must survive against the elements, and thrive with what we are given. The environment is the physical foundation for humanity and should be respected, but used, but not destroyed in its use. Our environment must be not be degraded for the purposes of sustainability and aesthetics.

We shape the environment and our environment shapes us. The environment includes the aesthetic of physical existence. Some aesthetics are better than others. Human beings create the aesthetic of cities, buildings, land, and existence. The aesthetic must be created with intelligence and planning. The aesthetic must first be compatible with complete functionality. Its construction must also get rid of chaos, artificiality and distraction. The distraction is a distraction from the fact that we live in a universe in which we do not know everything and are not in absolute control. Artificiality creates this distraction. The environment should not convey that humanity has taken over Earth, but is rather a part of Earth. Human beings do not need an environment of rigid order, but complete disorder is highly detrimental. A disorderly and chaotic environment creates a disorderly, chaotic, and destructive mind. An example of a contribution to a disorderly aesthetic is the street sign because it looks disorderly, and it is further destructive because it conveys a message of strict authority and order. I do not call for the complete elimination of all street signs, but care should be taken. Other examples of disorderly, artificial, and distractive contributions are large advertisements and logos, especially from corporations.

The aesthetic and environment does not have to be excessively planned or thought out to the extreme; this causes other problems both for the individual's mind in creating and in the creation of an aesthetic that is not that great and too artificial. The best aesthetic is created in the mind that is in a state of "pure creation"- supreme confidence and ability. The best aesthetic minimalizes the "dominion of humanity over nature" and infuses nature with functionality.

It is also vital to preserve the untouched natural environment in many areas large and small because we need the natural environment for its beauty, inspiration, and creation of wonder. Its beauty comes from being outside of human influence. The untamed environment serves as an example for what the universe without humanity would be like and the wonder that arises from this is invaluable and endless. The untamed allows for the individual to explore, become one with the universe, enjoy life, and feel wild. "Wildness is the preservation of the world" as said by Henry David Thoreau, and wild is what a real truth-seeker and builder must strive for.

Science

Science is necessary and important, but it is not holistic in answering questions or solving problems. It is dangerous for both direct and indirect reasons due to this.

Science is dangerous in direct ways. Science may appear to serve as a tool for the greater good of all, but it inadvertently may cause widespread destruction, especially in the hands of the wrong people. Technological advancements made from scientific thought in weaponry have caused widespread destruction and with the nuclear bomb, the possibility of complete annihilation. Harmful chemicals may be entering our bodies through plastics, the water, food, and other mediums. Through the scientific advancements made in the industrial revolution and continuing to today, we may be creating global warming. Artificial intelligence and genetic engineering may be detrimental to humanity. Other problems with technology are discussed in another section later on.

Science is also dangerous in an indirect way. For many people science is their guiding life philosophy, yet this is a shallow, incomplete, and dangerous way of viewing life. Science has become a maladaptive cult for many in our age because these weak-minded people reject the need to search deeper in the quest for truth and in this they remain in ignorance. This cult relies on science as a defense against meaninglessness, but in doing so it only creates destructiveness. Science is off the mark as a philosophy because rationality is not truth. The consequences of remaining rational are that it drives the mind and humanity into a constrained field of vision. The cult of science is heavily entrenched in believing that they are Right, and their ignorance has consequences. One must have a degree of irrationality and must make a leap of faith into subjectivity in order to understand the true nature of reality. Science does not answer all questions nor solve all problems, contrary to what many scientifically leaning thinkers may believe. A major problem with the cult of science is that these people reject the need to remain partially animalistic and power-seeking. The men of science are mostly physically and socially weak. There is no cultivation of masculinity in this cult and there is also no cultivation of femininity in women. The consequences of a loss of femininity are less severe than men losing masculinity, but they are still far-reaching. I wouldn't say that these unfeminine women instead are all masculine, but they are more likely to be. A reason why these scientific men are weak and confused, and women confused, is because they are all depressed. They believe in a deterministic universe, and this frame of mind destroys the individual. These people are also depressed for the obvious reason that they have some degree of truth-seeking in their nature, but with science there pursuits will automatically fall short to any real enlightenment or nirvana.

Despite the destructiveness in following and relying on science in the extreme, science is a very important tool in understanding the universe and accomplishing tasks.

Crime and Punishment

The origin of crime is free will and a feeling of powerlessness. The way we deal with crime should be a reflection of this.

Masculine men commit crimes when they cease to care about the world, when the world does not care about them, and when their freedom and masculinity are constricted. Of course the underlying reason is free will and powerlessness and this may directly be evident in the nature of the crime. A crime may be an act of pure free will in defiance of the artificial restrictions of society. Men are likely to commit crimes of pure destructive wrath because that is their nature. Men may also choose a life and livelihood of crime instead of leading a "straight" life because in the straight life their masculine nature is completely suppressed.

Society's solution to masculine men committing crimes is to simply remove them from society and not seek the underlying issue. Crime is a two way street in which it is ultimately the individual's responsibility for acting in destruction, but at the same time outside forces may play a role in pushing the individual. Instead of sweeping the issue under the rug and removing masculine men out of a feminine society, society must be corrected in allowing for the masculine nature to thrive.

A reason for the elimination of masculine men from society is because masculine men are the number one threat to the status quo elite. Masculine men, united, are the only people capable of overthrowing the status quo elite, so it would be in the power-hungry elite's best interest to get rid of these men instead of working towards solving the problem, because that problem is not a problem to the elite, it may be their creation. Gun control is another issue of the same nature. If the elite want to easily control a population, then gun control is the easiest way to keep the population compliant and weak. There is no hope for a physical revolution if the population has no guns. A weak feminine population of "men" and women with no guns will be incredibly easy to control and manipulate, and the people in power may go unchecked as long as the situation remains the same.

Women mainly commit crimes through deception because they desire power, but are not physically powerful, so they use other methods to get their way. A perceived lack of power pushes them to deceive. Women are manipulators and take advantage of their sexuality and perceived weakness to get ahead. Women who commit violent crimes may also "snap" and go mad due to mental weakness and a feeling that they are not getting their way.

Mental Illness

A whole new approach to how we think about mental "illness" is needed. There must be a philosophical understanding of mental illness, and the basis of philosophical understanding is understanding meaninglessness and free will. Free will and meaninglessness facilitate the formation of mental illness, so they should be the first area of focus in strengthening a mind. Mental illness is a response to either an unformed mind or a formed mind that becomes distraught and is breaking down. Mental illness is not really an illness but a breaking down of the mind by the individual self. The individual self may have been influenced by external factors, but in the end it is the self that is responsible for its demise. External influence may be needed in strengthening the individual's mind, but it is the individual self that is the only agent capable of driving oneself out of mental illness.

Free will allows the individual to feel, think and act in

any way possible. It is necessary to form a mind for a human being to function and enjoy life and in order to form the mind the allowance of all combinations of thinking or acting must be curbed. The goal of remedying mental illness should be to focus the person's thoughts to understanding, building, and order. The origin of all mental illnesses comes from the weakening of the mind through a lack self control, a lack of courage, a lack of wonder, and a lack of humor. Solve mental illness by encouraging the four ways of building- self-control, courage, wonder, and humor.

The Media/ Entertainment/ TV/ Music/ Internet/ Porn/ Advertising

Media (Mainstream newspapers online and print, websites, TV media, etc.):

The media has been corrupted by individuals whose only motive is to control, not enlighten. Society is being subverted and brainwashed through sedation, the pushing of degenerate and destructive ideas, and the pushing of pure ignorance. The subversion is completely overt to a person that sees the underlying motivation; disruption and control. Extreme care must be taken in gathering information by mainstream media outlets.

Entertainment:

Entertainment has become out of control and is used as a tool to subvert and control individuals of a society. Individuals' attention spans and ability to accomplish things are being eroded by a constant barrage of dopamine suckers, with the vast majority of society constantly looking at screens in a stupid dazed slumber.

Entertainment is a great part of life, but certain avenues of entertainment are not really entertainment at all. On top of this, entertainment should be experienced in moderation. The certain devious avenues are masked as nothing but entertainment, but in reality they are pure distraction and subversion. They are mechanisms of control. Other avenues of entertainment are a great way to escape the confines of life for a short while and experience the wonder of other worlds, or the wonders of this world, but a person that constantly pursuing these avenues ceases to face the realities of life and instead lives in fantasy and escapism, a destructive mindset. Entertainment may serve not only as an escape but as a distraction. The motive of the creators of certain entertainment may be to keep the viewers in a state of stupefaction, incapable of comprehending anything outside of their narrow and unexamined frame. The stupefaction and distraction of the viewer may only be the beginning, and may exist to prime an individual for deeper subversion- the true aim of most "entertainment". A person should be attentive to what they are being presented with and a person should control what they intake. Extreme caution should be taken in what a person feeds their mind, because what a person puts in is what they get out.

There is an entertainment value in watching sporting events in person, but demand for these events, and with this the price of a ticket to these events, has gotten out of control. Professional sports have gotten completely out of control. Any man who seriously cares about professional sports is a cuckold. Instead of worshipping athletic men, become an athletic man and become active. Play sports yourself. Professional sports have become a complete drain on society, especially on the mind and wallets of men.

TV:

Almost all of television is nothing but pure subversion and propagation in the worst way. This subversion and propagation is meant to weaken, stupefy, degrade, and control the masses to the benefit of those in power. TV is a medium of information transfer that creates pure passivity in the mind of the viewer. The TV lulls the brain into a sleep and the viewer is open to whatever information the screen emits. Television is not like a movie. An individual actively watches a movie by its nature and all of what the creator desires to convey is in a condensed 2-hour block. Television is mired in deception and the individual may view a series of TV shows over weeks, getting their weekly dosage of programming from the same creator each week with the more subvert "low dosage" hidden message being infused over a span of hours and hours. This is not to say that a person cannot be subverted by a movie. In fact people with malicious goals have controlled a large (and growing) percentage of the movie industry in the past and today.

TV is not entertainment and anyone who doesn't realize this is completely oblivious to the world around them. All of television is meant to program minds and unfortunately the creators of television use this power, without almost any exception, to maliciously program people to conform to their destructive agendas no matter how subtle or nuanced the agenda.

By doing away with television not only will the individual save an incredible amount of money, they will save their mind.

Music:

Music envelops and aligns the individual with its aesthetic. This aligning may be beneficial or detrimental depending on the nature and quality of the music and the time when the music is played. There is good music and there is garbage music. Music that is garbage propagates destructiveness and sedates the listener. Music that is good does not propagate destructiveness, awakens the individual, and enhances the individual in thinking and being.

There is a good time to listen to music and there is not. Constantly listening to music all of the time does not allow the individual to create their own existence and instead distracts. Always listening to music as a replacement to being alone in thought is detrimental, especially if the music sedates the listener. There is time for the enjoyment of good music and there is time to be alone in thought. A person who constantly listens to garbage, propaganda or not, exists in total subversion, sedation, and ignorance.

Internet:

The internet is a great tool for the sharing of information, but it comes with many harmful drawbacks. The internet pushes degeneracy, decreases attention spans, is an unhealthy medium for interaction between individuals, and overloads the individual with too much information, too much useless information, and too much destructive information. An individual should limit the amount of time spent on the internet and be in control of what they view on the internet.

Porn:

Porn is incredibly destructive to the mind of a man. Watching and masturbating to another man have sex with a desirable woman is an act of cuckoldry. The viewer is viewing another man have sex, or even if there is not a man in the video, the man is viewing something that he cannot attain. Masturbation may be necessary to release built up tension every once in a while (once a week, once every two weeks) if the man is not having consistent real sex, but pornographic material, especially videos, should not be used. Masturbating to pornographic videos, excessively or not, destroys a man's desire for real fulfillment and hinders his ability to achieve real fulfillment because it weakens the man. The man becomes programmed to enjoy the act of using his hand, viewing a screen, and viewing a woman enjoy sex with another man rather than enjoy the masculine affirming and fulfilling act of real sex. Through porn a man becomes hedonistic and over time views more degenerate material, deteriorating the mind. The hedonistic mind seeks further and further degeneracy because it needs more and more stimulation. Porn provides bottomless degeneracy. Degeneracy scrambles the mind.

Pornography is being pushed onto the masses of men

as a replacement to a healthy relationship with a real woman. This situation is partially women's fault for denying the access to sexual relations with the vast majority of men in favor of few, and is partially pushed by degenerate people in power as a means to weaken and control the male population; the only force capable of disrupting the current power structure if not in such a pathetic weakened state. Porn is creating a society of cuckolds. This is a citizenship of increasingly isolated, powerless and confused people, something very easy to take advantage of and control.

There is also a societal wide lowering of testosterone, the facilitator of masculinity. This lowering may be influenced directly by what men come into contact with. There may be estrogens in various mediums like plastics, food, and water that are lowering testosterone levels in men. Social factors play a major role. Porn also plays a role. Whether this lowering of testosterone is being done on purpose is unsure, although a population of weak men is easier to control.

Advertising:
Advertising is wasteful, it ruins the aesthetic of an environment, and it may be used to push falsehoods or as a tool of propaganda and subversion.

Advertising wastes enormous amounts of money pushing the masses into buy into the corporate economic scheme. What a complete waste.

Advertisements are the antithesis of a pleasant and inspiring environmental aesthetic. Instead of evoking the wonder of the universe, business advertisements evoke in people man's ability to ruin an environment. For the sake of the aesthetic, physical advertisements must be heavily done away with.

Advertising is used in our society to subvert destructive ideas into the minds of the population.

Advertising is an extension of corporate industry, media, television, and entertainment in terms of its subversion.

We must get rid of the vast majority of advertising, especially corporate advertising.

Lack of Freedom/ Technology/ Overpopulation/ Overcomplication/ Globalism

A Lack of Freedom:

There is an all-pervasive feeling and reality of a lack of freedom in our world, inflicting suffering and taking away the necessary power that each individual needs to enjoy life. The encroachment of freedom from outside sources is occurring on all fronts. We have government encroachment, technological servitude, overpopulation, overcomplexity, economic control, rules, regulations, strict social constriction, a lack of close-knit groups, and the list never ends. The trajectory that society is on will lead to the growing continuation of constriction and infringement. People are being driven apart and are being driven into submission and dissatisfaction.

Technology:

Technology helps people accomplish more, but it also weakens the individual and adds too much complexity that will disrupt and hinder lives rather than benefit.

People become dependent and weak when they use too much technology. Technology implies that it requires less effort to complete a task. Yet the point of life is not to complete tasks, but to forge a great creation and individual self. There is a lot of value in overcoming a struggle with only the use of the self and possibly limited technology. Without any struggle people become confused, weak, and hedonistic. The madness of our current society can be directly related to our society's heavy reliance on technology. Technology also takes away from life because it may provide an outlet for distraction. People are constantly thinking of new ways to entertain, sedate, and keep people occupied with fancy new technology. This distraction, along with the elimination of struggle is a serious disruptor to a truly enjoyable life.

The ramifications of technology permeate through all aspects of life.

Technology has taken over the economy and has put people out of work and subjected people to soul-crushing work involving technology. The best and necessary type of work is discarded for efficient work that turns a person into a cog in a machine. A person needs self-actualizing work that they find fulfilling. A person must be made strong and self-reliant in our harsh existence, not weak and reliant. The harshness of our existence makes life worth living. The difficulty in accomplishing tasks makes the completion of them that much more satisfying.

The environment is being destroyed and abused. The community has been eliminated as people stay in their homes, or may also travel far distances with ease. People work for giant corporations that heavily use technology, go home, sleep, and repeat. There is no community interaction or community interdependence; everyone depends on the machine. Technology has had devastating social effects. With its elimination of the small community, creation of large cities, creation of an extremely mobile population, and creation of the internet as a tool for communication with unlimited people, women can basically choose any man on the planet to have sex with, and she is free to have as much sex as she pleases. In the past a woman was part of a small community and was restricted in choice and experienced social curbing of degenerate behavior because everyone knew everyone. Now no one knows anyone, and women are free to roam the planet and have sex with anyone. This greatly increases the chances that a woman will be unlikely to settle down in the future with a man of equal sexual value, or that a man can even ascertain his standing in a woman's sexual past, because he most likely does not know her or know anyone that has known her for her whole life. People have also become reliant on technology to communicate, destroying the quality of their relationships rather than strengthening them. People need face-to-face real life interaction. Anything less than this is detrimental to the mind and to the cohesiveness of people in a society.

Technology makes our lives too complicated. We are unfulfilled. We are being distracted and forgetting to wonder. But there is a place for some technology in our lives. Technology plays a role in the actualization of exploration. There must be a limited and nuanced approach to the use of technology.

Overpopulation:

Overpopulation is a tricky situation. On one hand it is good for a population to reproduce. On the other overpopulation is a highly destructive world problem that deteriorates a society and affects each individual within and it is almost impossible to curb without taking extreme measures. Also add to this the fact that the most stupid and worthless people tend to reproduce faster than the rest because they do not understand the consequences, and curbing overpopulation with education becomes harder.

Populations that are not self-sustaining should absolutely not be artificially propped up from outside sources. A population of people that is dependent on outside sources will grow out of control and grow completely dependent. The population will need a continually growing support and will have a growing dependence for its sustenance for the rest of its existence. If a population is not meant to grow then don't make it grow.

Steps should be made to educate people on reproducing at a healthy balanced rate. There is another solution involving the alleviation of overpopulation by providing a release outlet in space colonization, which is part of my call for space exploration that I discuss later.

Overcomplication:

The world has become too complicated and too complex, making individuals feel lost, alone, and powerless. Life does not need to be complex, and a simple life is far superior. Society and systems within society must be scaled back and simplified. The truly important things in life must be brought into the forefront, and simplicity will follow.

Globalism:

We must simultaneously unite as a species, but exist separately in smaller identifiable distinct groups. Humanity must create and recognize smaller-scale groups such as races, nations, regions, smaller regions, cities, neighborhoods, and various groups for identity, understanding, anchoring, communication, self-reliance, and strength.

Each individual has more power and control if they are part of multiple levels of smaller and smaller groups that they can be a part of rather than be washed away in the masses. Identity is highly important in creating a sense of belonging, which is a subcomponent of both understanding and anchoring. With smaller groups the individual understands their place in the world better and can anchor (or work with) recognizable understandings and identifiers. Without these identifiers the individual cannot anchor on anything and is lost. It is far easier for an individual to develop closer relationships in which they can communicate with close people when these people are part of an identifiable group. With shared interest in one another and shared interest collectively, the smaller group is far stronger than a loose collection of human beings. Economically speaking these people can form a self-reliant and strong unit, which is beneficial in itself in its shielding of larger outside forces and in accomplishing things.

With globalism, all races are eliminated in favor of a mixed-conglomerate race, the individual is left at the mercy of the world economy and of the complexities of everything happening across the entire planet, and smaller groups are eliminated. Distinct races each bring something to the table of humanity to create a thriving diversity and each provide identity and belonging to each individual, something that a conglomerate race just does not provide. It may be thought in theory that a conglomerate race would still allow people to identify with and belong with the human race, but it is just missing something. It is not the same. The scale is too large and it is missing nuance.

The globalist economic structure inflicts an enormous amount of destruction onto all of humanity. With globalism, the businesses that pay their labor force the cheapest are the ones that thrive.

With globalism there is a lack of community. The community spirit has been driven out of existence by corporations taking over economically, and the spirit has been driven out by a pervasive thought that it is not needed. The community has been replaced by the larger global humanity, yet this is foolish. An individual must ground themself and strengthen and be strengthened by their community. Face to face communication and bonding is one of the greatest builders. Right after family, the community should be of great importance.

With this being said, it doesn't mean we can't unite as a species to accomplish goals like space exploration, preserving the planet, and worldwide understanding, cooperation and building while still remaining in our separate communities. But in order to combat all of the destructiveness in the world, and to combat existing alone in a meaningless existence, people must create smaller groups.

THE EXPLORATION OF OUTER SPACE

The Foundation is a foundation for the exploration of our existence in a holistic sense and also in a physical sense. The foundation for exploration is a foundation for the physical exploration of our universe. The physical exploration of the universe is a component of the holistic exploration of our existence in searching the unknown and providing structure to continue searching the unknown. Part of the purpose of all the foundations in building and preventing destruction is to provide a base framework for the continuing exploration of existence.

We must leave the (false) safety of the Earth and venture into the unknown and harsh universe. We must expand to the outer reaches of space and must colonize other worlds. The colonization of other worlds and manned exploration of deep space is the true exploration of our universe.

The true exploration of our universe is ingrained into the path of building and humanity must be on the path of building in order to truly explore the universe.

We must explore our universe to protect against complete annihilation. We exist in the cradle of Earth, but we cannot all remain here in one location because we exist in a universe of trillions and trillions of colliding and exploding chunks of various forms of matter so large and numerous that the mind cannot fathom our true place. Cosmic events are a part of a cosmic existence. A large rock, or star of bursting plasma, or black hole can hit or influence our speck of a planet at any moment without even a flinch from any one of Earth's inhabitants. It is time for every individual and the species as whole to know their place in the universe.

Nuclear war, global disease/environmental disasters, and overpopulation are other reasons for our species to expand off of one single location in which every member of our species is confined.

Space exploration and colonization solves the overpopulation problem. Our species can healthily reproduce in a seemingly infinite universe. If our universe is not infinite, or if it reverses its expanding nature and begins to collapse, overpopulation can be dealt with in other ways. The revelation of the universe's nature in those cases will provide humanity with something grander to consider and deal with rather than simply overpopulation.

Humanity needs courage, resilience, strength, and intelligence in order to explore space, striving for these things puts humanity on the path of building, therefore striving to explore space puts humanity on the path of building. The exploration of outer space is also a masculine endeavor, requiring men to be masculine and aligning them with the path of building. Especially in what I foresee in the shorter run, men must cultivate masculinity and use masculine traits to explore. Women will follow once the harshness of new worlds is reduced and new civilizations are put into place. Courage in a masculine sense is needed to explore, and is also needed to understand the need to explore. When men obtain masculinity, courage, and the spirit of exploration, it is paramount to explore to quench the masculine nature and spirit of exploration, and to keep men happy.

We must explore our universe to provide a goal for humanity to come together and work on. It is necessary for humanity to come together in order to accomplish real space exploration and space exploration provides something necessary for humanity to come together for. Space exploration has the potential to unite all of humanity.

Humanity always needs a struggle. We need adversity in order to create and build, otherwise people have nothing to overcome and life loses all value. The duality of human nature will always be a part of us and provide us something to battle with. The origin of the duality is the unknown and the unknown may always provide us a mystery to strive to solve. Space exploration is a continuing and never ending struggle because in the short term it is difficult, and in the long term with mastery we are provided with infinite space to explore and search. What exactly we must search for I do not know, but remaining on our speck does not help. If we do not try we will never know. If we do not find anything in outer space, then that is fine, we can remain in wonder. The exploration of space is not futile, just as building is not futile. If we do find something in outer space, just as if in our exploration of our existence we discover new knowledge, I do not know if anything I have said in this essay would matter anymore or not. This essay is not objective Truth; it is a subjective foundation for humanity given our current predicament and should be discarded when necessary.

Pursuing the exploration and colonization of outer space creates wonder in the individual and it is something that quenches the individual's need for actively pursuing wonder once it is created. It is our destiny to explore outer space if we decide to continue to exist.

If we do not look to the stars we will lose sight of life.

64385269R00071

Made in the USA
Charleston, SC
30 November 2016